T0064291

The Invisible World
and
the Visible World

The Invisible World
and
the Visible World

Where We Came From and Where We Shall Go To

Sukoun Choe

PARTRIDGE

A Penguin Random House Company

Because of the dynamic nature of the Internet, any web addresses or links contained in this book may have changed since publication and may no longer be valid. The views expressed in this work are solely those of the author and do not necessarily reflect the views of the publisher, and the publisher hereby disclaims any responsibility for them.

Print information available on the last page.

To order additional copies of this book, contact
Toll Free 800 101 2657 (Singapore)
Toll Free 1 800 81 7340 (Malaysia)
orders.singapore@partridgepublishing.com

www.partridgepublishing.com/singapore

Contents

Preface

Where did we come from and where shall we go to?

This question is very hard to answer. As we know, many philosophers, theorists and theologians have had tried to answer to this question from ancient era. As we talk about this question, term 'we' which is a collective noun have to changed to I, so this question becomes question of identity of me, a human being. In a word, the previous sentence is same meaning as the sentence "Where I came from and where I shall go to."

I am not philosopher, or physicist and my profession was a medical technologist. In my youth, I had hoped to study more to be a microorganism scientist, but my environment, the Korean school system, didn't give me a chance. So after graduation of college for medical technologist, I got a job at Maryknoll Sister's Hospital in Pusan city locatede in the south east of Korean peninsula as a medical technologist of clinical pathology depart for three years, after that times I had lived as a MT in medical field before beginning private business. After that time I had lived for about 10 years as a catholic man who had some questions of catholic doctrine. Also I had experience in manager of a small factory as a president for about twenty years, but at last my business failed and I became a poet about thirty years ago by recommendation of a late famous poet Mr. Park, Jaesam and a literature professor at the Hong Ik University Dr. Mun, Deoksoo via Poet Literature megagine. I have had the above question since the age of 17, the year of my father's death. In recent years I have had sorrowful experiences to meet several deaths among my family and friends So the above question made me study again with the view of religions, philosophy, and science. And a final opinion led to me writing this book which though small size, might contain new contents for my readers who have concerned this ultimate question of life. In Korea many older men would go to

Catholic Church to prepare for their last day. Most of them expected the last sacrament of the Catholic Church to lead them to heaven after death. How can we accept this social phenomenon for the young and the old of the world? But for many a man who have thought so deeply about such questions, there is no easy answer. In a certain point of view, this question belongs to the sentence of Socrates' "Know thyself" and Descartes' "Corgitto ergo sum". In the end to get some answers to this question, must come down to personal character of the way we perceive this world, so the proper knowledge of religions, philosophy, and science are necessary to understand basically the environment around us, because ultimately those answers are related to nature and the society in which we live. So I determined to write what I learned after researching for a few years to get some results for my friends who have similar doubts, which might be helpful to remember our peaceful and happy life.

Before writing this book, I had studied many religions, philosophy, biology and physics of myself to see such problems from the point of view of modern sense and knowledge with the special experiences found through religion. By the knowledge learned, I can infer some truth, and so I dare think it will be a first for my readers to read this work.

In Korea, there is a traditional precept coming down from generation to generation since ancient era, that is the Hongik-ingan spirit. The phrase meaning "For the good of humankind" is known to all Koreans as the rational spirit of building the oldest country of our people since about five to six thousand years ago. If we think about human's culture of that era, we must surprise that the old Korean's sprituality of high morality same as modern citizens. In fact, in our history, we can see the records in which they had had annual ceremony for thanks to the heaven and earth. I don't know the significance of dolmen without only archaeologial view point that it might be a trace of one of the tomb style about 8-2 centries B.C. like cromlechs or a trace of the religious ceremony in those era. In Korean peninsula, we can find many dolmens, but there is no castle like big constructions, so I assume that it might be used for religious ceremony. We can grant that the character of the culture and customs of a group of peoples must followed to the next generation by the habits and DNA of their own. Here I propose another evidence of the Korean people's DNA of religion for our ancestors' religion for heaven. Nowdays the worldwide christians surprised at the fastest increasing numbers of churchs in Korea in spite of short term after Korean War. I am sure that nobody can explain the reason of this phenomenon without the basic religional character of Korean's DNA to worship heaven [Hanullim, God]. And I hope to propose more detail exploration about dolmen to the associations of archaeologists worldwide. About the origin of the theme of **Hongik-Ingan,** I am sure that it was an Idea produced by those religional charater of our ancesters, and you can meet another evidence called **Chunboogyung** written below. I hope this book will become one in accord with our ancestors' idea, "For the good of mankind". After Second World War, the nationalism and the pure capitalism became the main idea to lead countries, under the modern political and economical worldwide environment. And the fact that many a church in the world has been losing their young believers, in the point of view that the future of mankind is belonging to the youths of the world, make us worried. So I have a thought that we need some one or some thing to relief this world before destroying all the value of human beings and natures on the earth. And that must be a some great one enough to embrace all beings in the world. Here, I write what I have explored about that being with various point of view. Let's call the being Hanullim or God, which have the specificity of spirituality, the greatest power and truth, and let's pursue the being whether we can believe or not via this work.

In past era, by the authority of Church it had been impossible for human being to discuss God, but now we can sure that the name of God was attached by human being for our convenience of recognition, so the abstractive being named God must never have the opposite opinion against our discussion, and let's give the will to relieve this world to God with spirituality. If we mankind expect some relief of God, that being must not be a abstractive existence but be a real being, because it is ought to be nothing but a image that have been showed by all of the philosophers and theologists, but unfortunately nobody give us the real evidence of God except the requisition of belief without any questions by the leaders of churchs. If God is not only but a image in our brain, we can not expect nothing to God, and if there were God in the sky as they said, though a trace of certain evidence could be showed us by the cosmophysicists with the best developed science. And so, I have tried to search for some traces of the reality with my physical hypothesis by myself, this book will show all that I have explored and the origin of exploration. And than, about the origin of my exploration, we can have such idea that if God have spirit to commune with human being, and if she need to show humankind some messages different from earlier era, and if she search for a man as a messenger, he must be a man who have great spirituality to worry about poor and painful men on the earth, and so it is possible for her to choice a man among the all humankind, among African, European, American, and Asian, because there is no comment at Bible to pick up one just among Israel, as a counselor who will follow to Jesus.

"In religion, however, each generation not only has to acquire theological insight of its own and in its own way, but it also needs to be in a continuing active dialogue with the generations that have preceded it, lest the specific insight that they attained should be lost. In particular, the adherents of a faith tradition have to remain in permanent contact with that tradition's unique foundational events. While contemporary theologians enjoy the opportunities provided by the particular perspective of today, they need also to seek to correct any distortion produced by that perspective by being willing to learn from the complementary insights of earlier generations. All firms of encounter with deeply personal aspects of reality have to take this historical dimension seriously, for the character of their understanding is not simply cumulative, and evaluations need to be made in a living relationship with the past."[1]

The sentences, showed above, written by J. Porkinghorne have significance in the view point of adaptation of religion to new generation, but I think that the truth is one which don't have any differences between generation to generation. And I don't agree with his opinion, showed below, as "In particular, the adherents of a faith tradition have to remain in permanent contact with that tradition's unique foundational events.", because the image of the word of 'tradition' must have the image of 'by human being'. So we can find the logical inconsequence at the word of 'tradition', because, in our history, many tragic accidents against human beings have had become justified by the word of 'tradition'. To tell strictly, 'tradition' do never belong to God, but belong to human beings having selfish mind. For example, as we know, all the accidents of anti-humanism and anti-life had happened in the both continent of Africa and America during 17 to 18 centuries by the believers of God. Certainly, we have to say 'tradition' do never belong to God. So we have to talk to our next generation not 'tradition', but 'truth'. I have thought that the faith tradition is the same as culture, which would be made by men having same thought and

---

[1]   J.Pokinghorne, Quantum Physics and Theology, Yale University Press, 2008,10p.

habits, and hoping to make group benefits, not by God. With this perspective, it is hard for me to understand below sentences. The truth of religion which was taught by the words of God, and by the faith of God, must be concreted, in spite of the differentiations of the times and the areas, and of the classes of mankind. So I think that it could be more acceptable to change the term of "faith tradition" to the term of "chruch tradition". And his opinion to search for logical sameness between quantum dynamics and macro-world is hard to understand as well, because, in particle physics, quantum phenomenon must be adaptable to the smaller world than the molecular sized materials. If quantum dynamic could be real in macro-world as his opinion, the regularity, the main specificity of nature will disappear, and we must live in the world of the complexed state with three dimensions and four dimensions, like chaos state. In a word about Quantum dynamics, it must be understood in a 'alternation phenomenon' from one to the other in course of forming electrons to be thought with origin of material in micro-world, though I am not physicist. It is true that all of the gross materials must belong to macro-world. Now, as human beings who live in globalized world, it must need the new morality for world citizens to get reasonable thought. The most men who had special experience to see globe at the artificial satellite, have said that there was no border between nations on the surface of globe. What do we must think after hearing the spaceman's experience?

1

Identity of me

1-1. I as a body

First of all, we have to identify that who I am and what I am, because I am a central being to recognize the relatives around me, to live with them on the earth, and in the space with many planets in the universe,

Generally we acknowledge that a man is composed of a body and a mind[heart and spirit]. This thought is very commonly regarded all by the people both eastern and western as truth. This dualism of the identity of a human being is accepted by all mankind. At first, let's think about our body which is understood easily by our reason, and let's look at the rate of my birth from a biological perspective.

a. Father side: There are approximately 100,000,000 sperm cells in 1 ml of male hormone, and usually 5 ml of hormone ejaculated at one time of orgasm.

The frequency of orgasm vary with age, but it is generally to have sexual intercourse one time per days of minus 1 from first number of their age as a proper interval for maintaining health. If we count the number of sperm cells ejaculated during a man's life, the number will be as follows.

100,000,000 x 5cc x {30times(20ages) x 12months x 10yrs + 15t(30ages) x 12m x 10yrs + 10t (40ages) x12m x 10yrs + 8t (50ages) x 12m x 10yrs + 6t (60a) x 12m x 10yrs} = 500,000,000 x 8280 = 4,140,000,000,000

= about $4{,}14 \times 10^{13}$

b. Mother side: Generally, females ovulate 1 ovum every month from the beginning of menstration to menopause. So the numbers of ovum adds up to the following:

12m (20a) x 10years +12m (30a) x10y + 12m (40a) x 10y + 12m (50y) x10y =480

c. If one has only one brother (or sister), the rate of one's birth is shown bellow.

$2 / 480 \times 4.14 \times 10^{13} = 1/ 993.6 \times 10^{13}$ = about $1/ 10^{16}$

While this number might be variable to personal difference, the probability of one's birth may be thought as the probability of finding a gold particle at the sand beach.

This body, as a frame of me, could hardly be born with such impossible probability. This body is formed in accordance with a natural congenital factor, called DNA and RNA which is passed down from parents biologically.

If we were composed of only body, we would be a puppet. We must understand this our body, because we can find out some connections between body and spirit.

1-2. Another I

- Inference for spirit as the other element of me

What do we think about the second element called spirit? Is it the mind or the heart? The time when a infant's independent life phenomenon showed in mother's uterus could be said to be the start in point of a human being's life. Here we can understand an individual life as starting from the heart, not the brain. Forthermore in vitro experiment under vital conditions, the pumping movement of the heart continued for a long time than the electric wave of the brain in physiology. We should give heed to this special vital function of the heart. In medical field, they identify death as the stop point of brain function, which means they can not prolong brain function but they can with heart function. So far, medicine has no answer to the question of how vital the first heart beat to an infant. We know that a cardiac arrest patient needs a very high voltage of direct circuit electric shock, but human's physiological electrical wave appears as only a mvolt unit. How can we understand this physiological phenomenon? As we saw above sentence, the heart is origin of life, in 2-3 months after the first heart beat, the brain can get action potential as a fetus in the mother's uterus. But we usually use the terms "mind" and "heart" interchangeably, without thinking of the biological origin. It is right to use the term "heart" as the origin of life, and the term "mind" as the origin of recognition as a brain function, and they both become the most important vital organs to preserve our life. But if we consider the relationship between heart and brain in the fetal period after 4 to 5 months of pregnancy, after beginning first heart beat, as time goes by, it can be said that the fetal brain cells become grown by the infant's blood circulation. Forthermore these brain cells are grown numerously to form a big brain like a globe with emotional and reasonal function.

Generally, they consider the two functions above to be mind, but it is reasonable to accept that the functions of brain appear after getting heart beat of body. The mind as represerved by the brain's action potential becomes critically important function to adapt to the changing environment around us in order to live.

Naturally this is a vital function of the mind, and this mind must adapt to preserve its own life. We call this the instinct of self-preservation. If it is hard to control this mind in the proper degree to live, naturally this mind shall be extended to preserve the body to the future. We call this momentum of mind, to want more than to live 'greed'. In a word, the cause of one's greed come from the fear and the anxiety of one's uncertain future.

To think deeply, the whole tragic history of anti-human accidents have happened due to this greed, as we know, national greed has been the cause of war, and some group's greed the cause of terror, personal greed the cause of murder. If we call either the heart or mind to be the spirit, it might be the heart because the heart has never had greed. Many theorists and theologians in the world have confused the mind with the spirit, so we must sincerely consider the true meaning of "spirit" to correct the word's concept and terminology.

Well then, what is this heart called spirit, and where does it come from? The answer to the question written above becomes the question of the identification of our heart and soul. Concerning this problem, many a philosopher from Socrates period to now have searched for the answer. In the bible there are several sentences said by Jesus that state "God is a spirit." Empiricists R. Descartes and I. Kant had tried to find the essence of God, the spirit in our mind, so now days we generally understand the mind as the spirit. For knowledge about this abstract existence, philosophy has developed into several fields such as psychology and brain science with a scientific approach, and physics has developed into astrophysics and particle physics.

We can say that our modern civilization is a result of Western rational, analytic thinking. Such thinking give us a good reasonable world, but sometimes it would become handicaps to understand another world. For example, we know that F. W. Niche insisted that we must have emotion and intuition to understand this world rather than a reasonable mind.

We have considered the physical "I" above. This physical "I", disappears with death which comes from the absence of biological electricity action potential.

Human beings have tried to find reason behind death. And so I have studied several religions and philosophy, and science to find an answer.

We have accepted that the other essence of a man is the mind (heart) or spirit generally after I. Kant by many philosophers, psychologists and human scientists. Here we must note the term "spirit" which is written as the essence of another "I", as a essence of God by Jesus' word several times in the bible.

By the 17 century, most of European had a theosophical opinion, but in 18 century, there appeared a new perspective of world, which become critical to the ecclesiology and theology of Catholicism. In particular, I. Kant, a great Deutch philosopher and empiricist based on empiricism, had an idea stating that we could understand world only with our reason. He thought that the ultimate, pure reason must be the essence of God. In other words, he thought the essence of God exist as our pure reason in our body. This means that God[spirit] exists in our body. Also his ethic showed in Kantian is similar to Lao-tzu's ethic, who was a oriental old naturalist, over Catholic ethic. And than, are they, the same, the two spirit, the human's spirit (mind) as God's spirit? The answer to this question will become the final result and the purpose of writing this book. If they are the same existence, Human beings are some special existence who can know the truth of this universe. Here we have to notice a modern great man, Suwoon, who declared the spirit in our body that is the essence of God after having a historical opportunity to meet Hanullim [Hanullim is the Korean name of God], on April 5th in 1860, at a small village in Kyungju province Korea. As Jesus and Suwoon said, if God is spirit itself, we have to try to understand the different point being between two great teachers.

2

To understand the identity and reality of Spirit [God, Hanullim]

If we write the idea stream of westerners, to Socrates' question in a sentence, Jesus said the man is an existence only to serve God[spirit] as a creature, and finally, by I. Kant, the answer changed to a existence of spirit[pure reason] in one's mind. After Kant, many philosophers have tried to find the essence of spirit through logical and scientific methods. In pure philosophy, Husserl and Whitehead, recent American philosophers showed us reality with their developed logical method, and brain scientists are trying to search the action potential of brain as an evidence of the spirit.

Nowadays, many physicists who have researched cosmology and micro-particle physics have tried to find evidence of the beginning of the cosmos and the origin of substance. Biologists and Biochemical scientists have indicated DNA of the nucleus chromatin in cells as the origin of congenital specificity in living individuals and species like us. With developed modern science and micro-biotechnology, mankind could make new life. But though their efforts have continued so far, they can't say what the reality of spirit is. If we look to our past, with the rationalistic tendancy of the Western world, who have developed modern civilization, the existence of God could be understood under the conditions of materialization of an abstract being. For the Eastern world, it has been difficult to understand this abstract being too, they have a concept called "Cheon" (sky / heaven) which is similar to the concept God as a hopeful standard of virtue and morality, which has been called Dao. But most Eastern Christians believe God as the Westerners have done. If so, how do we fully understand this term "spirit", the essence of God? It has been said that all believers of modern churches must believe a few miraculous accidents written in the Bible without any question, as they have learned by the leaders of religion in church.

I, as a writer, have searched for some men who have experience with meeting God as their beliefs are stated, in order to recognize the reality of the spirit more definitively via religions which have had special impact on their followers through out their history. We can know three of the greatest men in history who met God from their scriptures. Their names were Moses, Jesus and Suwoon. Muhammad is exampled because he met on angel instead of God according to the Sutra. But Moses didn't talk about the essence of God, though he received ten commandments. Only two men Jesus and Suwoon talked about the essence of God, as a spirit. I was very surprised to know that they said God and spirit the same.

I had compared with upper two men's scriptures, and their history of religion. As we know, from the Bible, Jesus was a great Man, born in Israel about 2015 years ago. Suwoon was a great man born in Korea about 160 years ago. They both had special experience to meet God, and they both said that the essence of God is a spirit in their scriptures. They both had 3 years of public ministry received from God to men, and they were both entrapped to die for their revolutionary teachings by jealous establishments. Also their favorite disciples, Peter and Haewol, both suffered honorable martyrdoms with reverence to their teachers. and many cases of martyrdom among their followers after their deaths. Those are showed in common by the invasion of foreign armies from Rome and Japan. These common historical facts happened seperated by 1880 years and a large geographical distance, from the Middle of Asia to East Asia. How can we understand this historical coincidence? But most Koreans, as well as world citizens in general have not concerned with such historical amaging similarity for long era. I have guessed the reason for ignoring this; It might be the dogmatic ecclesiology and theology of Christians to regard other religions as heresy without question.

I studied more about these two great teachers, Jesus and Suwoon, and there I came to know some differences about the essence of God [spirit] despite Suwoon's preaching that they are same "way" and "destiny" between Jesus' doctrine and Suwoon's doctrine. Before stating my opinion, we must first know the difference between two teachers' personalities. In the Bible we can find a sentence stating that Jesus had no chance to learn with scholars, which means he didn't have any knowledge of theology, philosophy and literature. Thinking educational environment of that era of middle Asia under the Roman rulers, and traditional education system of old Israel, we can't even be sure that he could read or write. According to the theologists, every sentences which he said in the Bible was written by his followers about 300 years after his death. But Suwoon had good chance to learn Confucian ideas, Buddhism, and others with several books because his father and grandfather were scholars of Confucianism as were most Korean scholars and governors at that times.(Chosun dynasty; 1860 A.D.) These different enviroment between their education, must have influenced their words and the way they perceived things, If so, it would be natural to have some differences in the way how they taught their followers with the messages which they had received from God. Now I will compare what they said about the essence of God.

In the Bible which was written by Jesus' followers, we can find the sentences in which Jesus said that God is spirit, and that he is light, a road and truth, and that he is alpha and omega. In Suwoon's scriptures, which are written by himself, we can find the sentences which show that God is spirit, (which we have too,) and that God is ultimate energy, and that God is truth which is no law of no return. We can unsderstand that Jesus' "light" is the same as Suwoon's energy, than these three essences of God are common between them. About truth, Jesus did not comment any more in detail. He only showed us the 'alpha and omega theory', which is thought of as the beginning and ending by most of man- kind as showed in a linear world. But we know that God is not a being of the first or second dimension. We must have a higher dimensional idea for understanding the sentence of 'alpha and omega', and I dare say that the above sentence written at the Bible must be understood as a circlulation theory with a round and spiral pattern with the three or higher dimensions.

Those who agree with this idea can understand that the truth which is written in the Bible is the same meaning as Suwoon's doctrine. Most Christians' an apocalyptic view of history is originated from misunderstanding the truth which have been retranslated with slightly different meanings from the time the the Bible was written until modern era without any deeper thought about reality.

Forthermore most Christians think of the spirit to be a cosmological being only, while Suwoon said that all beings of nature have a spirit and the cosmos are filled with spirit. If we compare the above sentence with theological word, the sentence in the Bible becomes a monotheistic idea, and the sentence written by Suwoon (who said this truth was given by God) becomes the monotheistic and panentheistic idea in common and in the same time, regarding all creatures to have a spirit. How shall we understand these different aspect of spiritual existence? Thinking of the very similar religious history between these two men selected by God, I dare say that the difference in understanding could have appeared due to the difference in each era's background, civilization and culture, which influence man's ability to recognize.

All the men, in this world, have had thought God is an abstract existence in nature, but if Suwoon's doctrine were true, the existence of God might be a reality.

Having such an idea, I have tried to find out some evidence of his reality through science and philosophy.

We have observed the communication of emotion between human being and animals by zoologists and by our experience of living with them. And with the evidence of electromagnetic experiment, many botanists accept the fact of the communication between human being and plants. According to the some of American botanists having such experience, he could find such phenomenon occur even when seperated by the distance of hundreds of miles. Considering these experiments, it is right to assume that human beings can communicate with all forms of life. From a scientific perspective, all life is sustained through the electromagnetic mechanism of action potential from cells to cells and cells to mater. Lack of change is the state of death. Our mental capability of cognition occurrs by these action potential as well. If it is thought to be an electromagnetic mechanism that communicates between human beings and other life forms, there must be a electromagnetic wave connecting among them. But human beings have only weak electrical waves measured in the mm voltage unit. Therefore our bio-electricity can not across far distance of hundreds of miles like broad casting wave. Well then, how we can understand the experiment of botanists and zoologists?

We know the Higg's particle via science media, many physicist have argued over the existence of that particle. At last CERN acknowledged the existence of Higg's particle with the experiment performed by some physicists, and with the method of mathematical account on Oct. 2013, and they can be proud of winning the Nobel Prize. They said that this Higg's particle might be the first origin of substance in the world, which have special function of connection intra standard model of particles, some of them called this particle God's particle because they hypothesized it as the matter present at the first moment of creation.

If they were right, the final identity of God would be Higg's particle, however we can't be sure of their existence yet. Here we have other questions; what is the origin of the particles' connected by Higg's particles? And is that the most basic existence in physics? Such evidence of the origin of existence have used only a mathematical approach comparable with the philosophers' approach of logical deduction. Apologies to the physicists, but we have no evidence of the origin of creation. The claim of their existence is only a claim of some scientists. They must answer the question "By way of the Higg's particle, can we communicate with animals and plants?" Because this question is very important for us to understanding God's specificity that is spirituality, to create life, cosmos and preserve lives and universe without stopping for a moment. And ultimate question is that "Can we think the particle which can be checked with light absorption film, to be spiritual creator as the origin of matter?"

2-1. Physics from the point of view of the mam-factor hypothesis

A. Exploration of the existence of mam-factor

In Greek, the ancients had thought 'aether' to be a substance of personification of a clear air of the sky, and this idea coming down to the modern physics as a hypothetical substance supposed to occupy all space, postulated to account for the propagation of electromagnetic radiation through space. I suppose that this old Greek's idea that some personification might exist in heaven on the sky become basic idea of the Christianity, of which God might live in heaven on the sky. About existence of ether, in spite of Michelson-Morey's experiment, Albert Einstein, pointed out that the whole idea of ether was unnecessary, providing one was willing to abandon the idea of absolute time.[2]

---

[2]   A BRIEF HISTORY OF TIME, Stephen Hawking, 1988, Bantam Books, 20, 23.

But, instead of ether, from now let's assume that there exists a very fine particle-like spherical structure with the character of a very fine soup bubble and like a coccus of microorganisms sized 10^{-40} (a questionable constant number in particle physics to be accounted by some physicists), and that they exist in the pattern of grapes, like the grapes shape visible at the very early growing cell division stage of a fertilized ovum with one membrane attached to the others, and they fill all of the space from between nucleus of atom to a universal scale.

Here I use the words "membrane", "wall" and "border" as the term borderline to identify the image of the barrier between factor and factor, because there is no proper word with human's recognition so far. It might be the smallest trans electro-magnetic curtain to isolate each other, with the utmost flexibility. Most of physicists have wondered what the super micro size number of 10^{-40} means(They said that this number have appeared constantly with mathmetical account in particle physics.), if such utmost fine beings were in the world, we can never see it forever with our eyes. Human Beings could never feel it, and so humankind would never recognize the existence of such tiny being that have not yet been found by particle physicist. For understanding the existence of this fine factor, let's think in reverse order under the hypothesis of existence of such fine structure, and let's call this super micro being a "Mam-factor". The reason why I call it "factor" in stead of "particle" is that it would have some special characteristic different from a simple particle in physics. And than, let's think again microphysics, physical laws explored by physicists. If we could assume that the cosmos are filled with these factors, then we have to change our view point about the origin of everything- substance, life, and cosmos,- which we have any provious idea about.

First of all, let's look at the electron, proton, and neutron under the condition of this hypothesis.

If we assume that the constant number of 10^{-40} is the weight or size of an utmost fine factor, a electron granule would be composed of the factors of 9.1×10^9.

[9.1×10^{-31} Kg (wt. of electron.)/ 10^{-40} (wt. suggested that utmost fine mam-factor would be constant unknown,) = 9.1×10^9]

This calculation means that one electron would be composed of 9.1×10^9 numbers of mam-factors. (Here, pleural form used only for grammar, It is natural to use the term of mam-factor as the term of water, one of substantial name because we never can separate one from others.)

These factor would have little energy of movement, despite this very fine structure. By some very little stimulation around them, like temperature or the force of gravity, positional energy, or electro-magnetic power, they would move easily. If they were surrounded by an electro-magnetic barrier, it would be easy to form clusters of themselves and therefore become the origin of alternation.

With this mechanism, the cluster could be formed with 9.1×10^9 mam-factors, and we could call this an electron. This electron state would become the most important of all. It might become the origin of all of the materials in the universe.

It might become a proton, neutron, atom, molecule and formed material by influence of inner and outer forces. At last they could become the origin of this world and universe. If we think twice, that fine factor could become the utmost origin of all organism and non living things, because every structure in the universe is made of atoms composed of protons, neutrons and electrons.

Exploration of the photon

Photon would be the name of the particle of light, which was approached by Albert Einstein, one of the greatest physicists in the world. In spite of his the greatest feat serving mankind to understand universe via relativity theory, some point of his view about photon and anti-particle is hard to accept to me.

If the universe were filled with finest factors [utmost fine being sized 10^{-40} that can not be called particle] in the space of universe, the power of explosion could make some wave, because the specificity of power transferring through the finest factors might have resistance of fluid dynamics as a starting submarine under the surface of the sea must make waves of water though non seen. I think the velocity of the transference of this original power will be determined and influenced to the count of waves, height of wave, and wave length.

Here, I have to talk about the specificity of the mam-facter's character that I have thought again, at first it might be a the utmost fine size and weight with the finest space about 10^{-40} kg/meters(this unit of universal constant is not identified yet by physicist's mathematical counting) with the capsule of very small clear soup bubble which have elasticity, and second it might have spiritual character that can commune to the lives(as some physicists recognized some being to commune with human in this space), third this cosmos might be filled with this fine factors as if the ocean is filled with and composed of water molecules, fourth it might have continuous self-divisional capacity autonomously like the division function of virus like microorganisms, for this reason, the cosmos would have to enlarge without stopping, and it might make the time and space with the increasing account to the unknown margin of cosmos, fifth they might have the functional reliability of changing from one dimensional to three dimensional character physically with four dimensional function of spirit.

If we mankind could have some evidence of reality of this utmost fine mam-factor, and we could have some technique to check out our mind physically some day, we could know that our mind might have the greater velocity than the light wave to transfer through the space without any resistance because our mind might be a same quality with this mam factor. Here, I dare say that the utmost fine factor would be mind factor[spirit factor: heart factor] as a character of God[Hanullim]. In the world of spirit[heart], as we know that there is no any barrier to isolate each other, and any distance not to correspond, if want. And in fact, we can read that some physicists had the experience of existence of some factors to commune with human mind during his experiment of light wave. Generally we learned that the electron particle can have circulation movement around the nucleus by itself for gravity force, but I dare think the electrons only can be understood by the moving stream of mam-factor's layer to be limited to the border line formed by faster circulation velocity among them and by the gravity of nucleus, as the very fine particles of soil that can move autonomously by the air streams itself[with the particle's specific movement] in the balloon. Because the mam-factor might be a utmost small in size and in weight, they might have move always without fixing state just like water molecules under the sea, and so by the some stimulant force of energy among them they will make some wave patterns of response to the stimulant and the wave will spread to the all directions. If my opinion would become true, on thinking this stream flow character of mam-factor, we could say not "the electron's movement of circulation" but "the energy creation to be caused by the cluster of the circulating mam-factor." In this point of view, it become easy to understand quantum theory and some questions of physics, I would think so. Here if we think energy, we can find a power in fast circulation movement of fluid with the outer barrier. More over if they would go round faster to the one direction in globe shaped borderline formed by some differentiation of electromagnetic charactor, and go round faster in circular movement formed by some electromagnetic phenomenon, there will appear spiral pattern movement of each mam-factor. About the globe form border, I dare think that, by the gravity theory of Newton, a atom's nucleus might have some space around with constant diameter. In that space might have difinite amount of mam-factor, accoring to the length of the diameter which was made by the contractive power of nucleus gravity. This means that, according to the nuceus gravity, the amount of mam-factor will be determined, and it will definite the diameter of globe. Finally, I dare say that the numbers of electron will be determine with the amount of mam-facter. If we accept this thought to the universe, we can enlarge to the great volume of mam-factor's tornado, and it will make a big power enough to make cosmic absolute vacuum state in the center space. And it might be called a black hole, to which all things are aspirated, because it might have the utmost aspirating power due to the absolute vacuum state of center, which is formed by the utmost spiral circulating with the universal scale power of mam-factors' layer, that might have electromagnetic specificity. If we think about mam-factor in detail, I dare assume that below specificity.

Identity of mam- factor in my hypothesis

1. Mam-factor may not be a particle but factor with very fine size of 10^{-40}.
2. Mam-factor may have 4 dimensional being having the specificity of substance, and spirit.
3. We have to define them not only to be substance but to be super-substantial being, so they can not be written with pleural noun to be attached with s or es.
4. "Anti-matter" in physics must be changed to the "mam- factor".

5. Two kinds of unit would be recommended for using quantity unit of mam-factor, one is the unit of emf [3] in physics of material world, and the other is unit of lmf [4] in biology of life world.

The following contents could support the hpothesis of the mam-factor.

1. Logical reinterpretation of photon theory
    (logical exploration with three stages)

A) In quantum theory

   1) Quantum theory can be understood as the movement of particles less than electron size.
   2) If we accept that the photon might be a particle which was insisted by some physicists, there needs energy to break the particle substance.
   3) There is no evidence of increasing energy just before photon's disappearing.

B) Photon particle theory

   1) Particles do not change its physical character in the different time and space.
   2) If photons were produced by the light source, it must be observed that photon shall be increased in universe.
   3) There is no evidence of photon particle's increasing after loss of light.

---

[3]   emf: the electronic unit of mam-factor: the proper amount of mam-factor of which power could create electronic wave.
      (1 emf is suggested for 9.1×10^9 numbers of mam- factor. ref: 13 p)
[4]   lmf: the life unit of mam-factor: the proper amount of mam-factor by which power the first heart beat can start.
      (It is hard to calculate numbers of mam- factor so far. Let's suggest that 1 lmf must be a power producing first beat of infant's heart in mothers womb.)

C) No photon is in the universe

   1) There is no evidence of increaisng energy just before ptoton's diappearing in the micro world.
   2) There is no evidence of photon particle's increasing after loss of light in macro world.
   3) Photon particles might be abstract image that insisted by a part of physicists.

2. Reinterpretation of identity of the light

   1) If the photon of light really existed, it would too small to be perceived by human's optic nerveous receptor.
   2) If light were a particle and a wave in common as Einstein insisted, it must be interpreted that how the variations of particles change according to the wave lengths of 7 colors of optical light.
   3) So, with my hypothesis, I dare insist that the light is horizontal waves composed of the mam-factor's clusters, which produced by the resistance of the original energy against the mam-factor filled in the space, as it is known that a transfering phenomenon of the original force among the fluid, just as the water waves composed of water clusters, and of which lengths can be perceived only by our optic nerve among the several lengths of waves.
   4) So it is more reasonable to use the term 'photove(photo+wave)' instead of 'photon' when talking of in quantum physics, which might form with velocity of mam-factor's movement in atom globe. Because it is same as we can't say 'water wave' to be 'water molecules', in this case, we can recognize that 'wave' is not 'molecules' but 'movement' formed by the fluid's resistance to the power moving forward with the phenomenon of the fluid dynamics.. And so with the same reason, 'light' is not 'particles', but 'wave', and with this reason, all the waves found in the universe might be said 'the waves of mom-factor, which is created by certain original force of energy going forward.

3. Reinterpretation of quantum theory

So far, the most physicists have thought that the 'quantum' might mean the quantum phenomenon of particles, but I think we have to change this identity of 'quantum' to the idea of 'quantum of the movement power of mam-factor' [here we can't use 'factors', because factor is material like water not to be counted.]. Such reason that we have to change the identity of quantum, is that 'quantum of particle' can never get energy of movement but gravity and positional energy, and so it could be understand below relation of equations.

1) $G = mm' /r^2$ ---Newton's law
2) $E = mc^2$ ----Einstein's law
   m: weight of mam-factor
   m': weight of nucleon

In atom, if there are same as G=E, outer capsule of mam-factor can never protect nucleon, so atom might loss the capacity of self-exsistence. For a atom's existence, it might need very outer protector, and the relation between nucleon and protector must be relationship of the state of below equation.

$mm' /r^2 < mc^2$
$1 < c^2 r^2 / m'$

As it showed upper equation, electron might appeared when the energy of circulatory motion of mam-factor become larger than quantum of it. Accordingly I dare propose that it might be proper to use the term of 'quantum forming of circulation energy theory' than simple 'quantum theory' to physicists. Because the image of 'quantum' do not mean moving energy, but as the relativity that Einstein said have showed, there is non moving substance in cosmos, and with the energy of gravity and position, it is impossible to interpret this universe. And if we can accept the truth of regularity of alternation in nature, it might be possible to appear the quantum phenomenon with some regularity, because we know that the preserving conditions of atoms might be constant, even though the confirmability producing electrove could be very hard to account, due to the numerous case of forming waves, and numerous size of waves of mam-factors in the atom.

4. About Dark Matter and Dark substance in the cosmos

    1) Dark material and dark substance might not be material and substance, because no evidence has been found yet of material and substance.
    2) Dark might mean a space with no light waves in cosmology.
    3) They might be trunks and branches of broken **absolute vacuum space** scattered by big bangs, which might be the mam-factors' giant cosmic tornado formed by their electro-magnetic circulation movement as written below.
    4) Therefore the Dark spaces might be made of the strongest pulling force created by the specificity of an absolute vacuum state of a mam-factors tornado. That would absorb all the mam-factors causing wave around it, and they would seem like dark material and substance. So the dark field might be non-mam-factor field, because the light wave can never formed without mam-factor.

5. Logical reinterpretation of anti-particle theory

    1) In physics, there is the law of stating that the total quantity of matters be never changed before and after some alternation in the macro-world and in the micro-world in the universe.
    2) If the anti-particle did exist, it would dissolve not only particles, but matter and the universe itself, so we must make a choice one of two theories written above.
    3) So we can say that the concept of the Anti-particle is only imagination of some physicists. With the result of deep insight, there is no anti-particle and no anti-matter in the universe.

6. Reinterpretation of Einstein's equation

    (1) On the formula of $E = mc^2$

    C (velocity of light) could be accepted in case the identity of light was a particle, but if we were to change the identity of light to a wave, c must be changed to (wn/t) as below,

$E = m \ (wn/t)^2$,

w: The amount of integrated energy in one light wave's volume, which is formed of the mam-factor filled in the universe.

n/t: The number of total light waves counted in total distance during one second.

(2) If we think about Einstein's equation again, It might be correct to change the image of $E=mc^2$ to the image of $P=mc^2$ because the unit of equation must have great significance, for example, if we multiply the velocity to the weight, the result must be the image of power. In our common sense, for being energy unit, it needs that one of two factors to be multiplied has energy unit, as I wrote above.

7. A diagram showing relationship between mam- factor and universe

    1) time/space

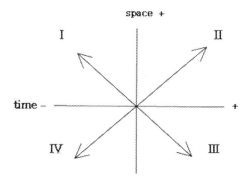

* Left graph might show the relationship between space and time, but such alternation have appeared in the cosmos with the 5th dimensional pattern, so it could appear simultaneously the 4 alternations (I,II,III,IV).

* Space: Concept of the volume (amount) of mam- factor increasing. Time: Concept of count (number) of mam- factor dividing.

With this mam factor's hypothesis, time and space is two different images of mam factor, and so upper graph showed, the direct line of y=ax and y=-ax of I, II, III, IV dimension must be patterns of mam factor's state in universe. Accordingly, the basic point (0,0) might become the image of the absolute vacuum state of pre-greatest first big bang event. Upper 4 alternative state of space/time might happen consequently at several part in all universe, as 4 seasons on the earth, and we could understand that there is no absolute time/space in universe as Stephen Hawking insisted.

2) Universe

a) ultimate concentrated central material

b) dark vacuum field, out of the great universe.

c) spiral circulating mf in the great universe

d) benting and curling area into e) (I. III)

enlarging universe (II)

e) ultimate vacuum tunnel formed by cosmic tornado of mf turning around. (IV)

a: The ultimate concentrating nucleus material with a great heat formed by the absolute vacuum's power, and with a great cold made by the greatest absorbing power created by the universal spiral circulating movement of mf filled in the entire universe. This heating mechanism would be the origin of big bang, and by the huge explosion of this great concentrated nucleus, being the origin of the Big Bang would have made the next universes.

b: The huge Dark field might exist all around the great universe. This area might be a vacuum state without mf because if there were mfs, scientists could find some trace of light visible by the wave of mfs. It could be guessed that the great universe would be enlarging more and more for this vacuum state, which have negative pressure, could absorb the margin of the great universe formed with mfs.

c: This spiral circulating movement could be understood under the condition accepting the mfs hypothesis having the special specificity of electro-magnetic character becoming moving energy.

d: The mf's curling area might be formed with whirling mf to be bent and absorbed into the central vacuum tunnel axis connecting both poles just like the central space of tornado.

e: This ultimate vacuum tunnel formed by the cosmic tornado of mfs turning around of entire universe, leads to the central vacuum tunnel axis connecting both poles. When the extremely hot material in the center explodes for over-heating, this could be called Big Bang accident occuring at this stage, and the debris of the broken axis of the vacuum tunnel might be scattered into the surrounding space along with a great volume of mf, and so finally many small universes could be created with the debris of the original great vacuum tunnels at their center. Furthermore the small universes might become filled with mfs, and they might explode on a smaller scale as well, due to the same mechanism as written above. And so we can call these smallest universes and the galaxies. According to this hypothesis, there might be many middle universes containing many galaxies which have various size black halls just like organisms having tissues in our body. At last the swelling and growing mechanism of universe might originate to the Big Bangs created continuously here and there in the universe filled with mf.

B. Mam-factor movement in the atom

-quantum phenomenon forming electron.

Let's think of the spherical shape globe composed of mam-factors with the electromagnetic layer formed by the gravity of a nucleon. The first straight movement, will become the two directions of stream, one is the stream flowing toward inner from outer, the other is the stream flowing toward outer from inner by the reflection. These two streams must make a special circulatory movement of spiral pattern mixed with many size diameters' circulation, autonomously, continuously by the circulating power and the gravity. These special patterns of fluid dynamic movement can make many waves, with many directions formed by the numerous resistance, produced by striking each other, and to others, and reflecting onto the curved wall. With this phenomenon, there must be occurred the coincide or cancel patterns of wave crests irregularly in limited space. If there formed some coincide pattern of waves, it will be a momentum of enlarging energy patterns, here I dare think this might be the "momentum of appearing electrove (electronic wave: elctron called)" and the "momentum of photove(light wave: photon called)".

This enlarged energy integrating power of coincide waves must have some power of potential energy naturally, it will make energy increased to the central particles called nucleon to become a protective barrier ot preserve its own structure. Finally, thus we could find the atomic structure as the original matter of substances in this world. If the energy balance accomplished with gravity and circulating movement of mam-factor could be broken, it would need bigger energy momentum of circulation energy of mam-factor forming spherical pattern. If we think the atom's character with the hypothesis above mentioned, the hardness of atom would be changeable according to the number of electrove. Because the quantity of coincide waves might be proportional to the amount of mam-factor, and to the degree of nucleon 's gravity. If some atoms would have more mam-factor, according to the central nucleon's gravity, they will get more amount of coincide waves to form electro-waves, and they become harder and harder, for example, the carbon atom is harder than the hydrogen atom and hydrogen atom is harder than helium atom. (ref: experiment for fluid dynamics in globe)

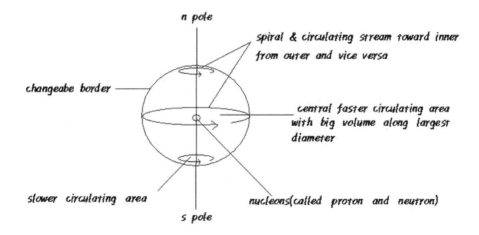

n pole

spiral & circulating stream toward inner from outer and vice versa

changeabe border

central faster circulating area with big volume along largest diameter

slower circulating area

nucleons(called proton and neutron)

s pole

To understand the relationship of energy, it might be possible to think according to the following figure and equation.

$G = mm'/r^2$ - Newton's law

$E = m(wn/t)^2$ - -modified Einstein's law (with mam-factor hypothesis) (*ref.:25p)

In atom, balancing state of power to preserve atom's frame

$G = E$, $mm'/r^2 = m(wn/t)^2$

$\qquad m' = (wn/t)^2 r^2$

$\qquad$ m': wt. of nucleon

$\qquad$ m: wt. of mam-factor

$\qquad$ (mam-factor's quantity of in on electrove, written) above)

$\qquad$ r: distance from nucleons to the middle point of atom ball that is average value of spiral circulating mam-factor's stream not just half of radius of globe)

$m' < (wn/t)^2 r^2$: time point that electrove appear

$\qquad$ (when mam-factor's circulation power is larger than gravity of nucleon, gathering mam-factor from the surrouding space,)

$m' > (wn/t)^2 r^2$: time point that electrove disappear

$\qquad$ (when nucleon gravity is lager than mam-factor's circulation power, scattering mam-factor to the surrouding space)

This balancing could be changeable for mam-factor's circulating movement being constantly, so electroves might appear very irregularly, this phenomenon might be called quantum phenomenon.

Figure: The energy of spiral circulation mechanism of electro-wave appear with circulation of mam-factor in atom.

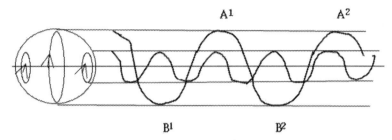

Figure: Coincide(A¹,A²) and cancel(B¹,B²) phenomenon of mf's waves in atom. There might become a point of electronic power appearance in case that a certain point of which the total energy integrated from A¹ to Aⁿ minus the total energy integrated from B¹ to Bⁿ become larger than the gravity of nucleons. I dare think that this phenomenon might be quantum theory which they have called

As shown in the above figure, a central border plate might appear along the longest central circulation stream which formed by special spiral curling movement of mam-factor filling the balloon like outer border toward both inner-pole side from outer-center dividing the atom sphere into two parts. And then sometimes, one or two electrons irregularly appear, each adjust to it's own hemisphere by the gravity formed in the space filled with mam-factor.

If I wrote the relationship of mam-factor to the cosmos, it could be showed as below.

mf: mam-factor   n: nucleon   e: electron   a: atom

m: molecule   s: substance containing cells   e: earth

ss: solar system   mg: milky galaxy   u: universe   c: cosmos

$$mf \in e \in n \in a \in m \in s \in e \in ss \in mg \in u \in c \in mf$$

Here we can see the relationship of one function to the others. Each of the functions showed at every stage of directional progressive alternation is a constant function with constant mam-factor. The grand unified field theory, which physicists have tried to find, could be understood with the above equation of the hypothesis of the existence of mam-factor, in other word, the grand unified field could be understood as the whole world of this cosmos containing visible and invisible world.

In this point of view, the atom's capsules which have been insisted by the phisicists could be thought to be layers of mam-factor which formed in proportion to the gravity of central nucleons and to the circulating energy of mam-factor's stream. For example, a helium atom might be very unstable having insufficient gravity to hold insufficient amount of mam-factor, because an atom which has only one electrove(electron), despite that the symmetric specificity of intra circulatory movement of mam-factor ought to form dual electroves(electrons), must be unstable.

2-2. The experiment for fine particles' movement in water globe.

1. Purpose of this experiment
What the rotating water stream will be showed in globe filled with water? (or how the fluid dynamics will appear in globe?)

2. To prepare

a. Instrument

    1) two hemisphere glassy acryl ball with 3mm depth
    2) tap water
    3) soybean powder
    4) iv-set, and syringe
    5) central bar with crank style handle, attached thin wing(about 2x7cm, for making circulation movement of water in the globe

I - 1   I - 2   I - 3

3. Procedure

    1) Make an acryl globe with the two hemispheric acryl and silicon, which contains a central thin copper bar attached thin aluminum plate, by 2cm x 7cm with crank style handle.

    2) Insert tap water into the space of the acryl ball near full with iv-set, and insert again the dilluted corn powder with the syringe,

    3) Rotate copper bar handle slowly.

b. Result of Experiment

    1) On beginning rotating handle of central bar with aluminium wing slowly, the fine soybean granules flew up through the longitudinal central plate area along the ball wall, and curved forward, and than two streams of fine corn granules appeared at both side of central round water plan, and at last it became diffusion state, with the spiral movement and with various streams mixed up. [ref.: I-1, I-2]

    2) In the same method with millets, the millet stream divided to two streams before diffusion state as the above experiment in case of using the corn powder, and gathering phenomenons appeared in both area of bar fixed, and they are scattered in few seconds. [ref:I-3]

c. Significance of this experiment

    1) In globe, fluid dynamic must form the wave for their spiral movement from outer to inner, and from inner to outer, and finally there was no straight movement in globe. Generally the current must be mixed up.

    2) Despite of this mixed state, very occasionally the spiral and circulatory movement will appear with two main streams along the longist diameter and it will form both hemispherical circulatory and spiral streams though it would be just a moment. This must be a momentum of forming electrove(electron).

    3) If we think of the self rotation phenomenon of the earth, as the same fluid dynamic movement of the magma showed above, we can suggest the contents written below.

Hypothesis of self-rotation mechanism of the earth

Under this hypothesis, we can also find the occurence of similar phenomenon, like the atom-like movement of the daily rotation of the earth, forming a circular movement of hot fluid magma is similar to the spiral and circulating movement as mam factor's stream in atom. Circulating streams of semisolid hot magma would make main stream power along the longest inner diameter of the earth, which form the two largest circulations sometimes, which divide magma to two main streams, circulating from west to east, and it make self-rotation axis on the right angle direction to the center of central circulation plate produced by circulating magma along the longest diameter direction of globe.

Accordingly, if it happened that the longest inner diameter changed by the partial solidification, or by the other origin, and the direction of this great circulating power could change, and than new circulation axis will formed with the right angular direction. So I dare suggest that the slope of 23.5 degree of rotation axis to the right angle of outer pattern of globe had been formed by this ellipsoid pattern of inner layer of earth. Following to this phenomenon, the earthquake and volcanoes' explosion might be understood of appearing phenomenon by the circulating magma beneath the earth surface. And if we guess the reason why the slope of axis of globe formed, it could be understood with the eccentric magma circulation which is caused by the different thickness of superficial layer of the earth during one old era. And I dare think, if we could make magma into the center of the moon, it will have faster self rotation movement and the bigger gravity.

Figure: The hypothesis of self-rotation movement mechanism of the earth caused by similar magma movement like fluid dynamic movement of mam-factor's movement showed in the atom with this hypothesis. (ref: the experiment of fluid dynamics in globe written above.)

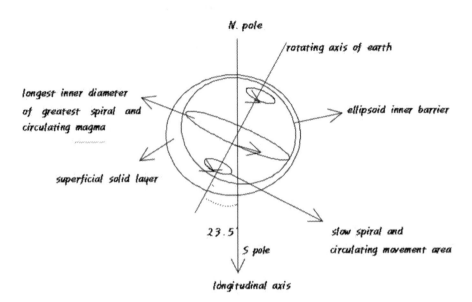

If some evidence of self-rotation of globe as the hypothesis written above could be identified by the globe-scientists, and than we can understan mam-factor's theory explorated with same hypothesis of fluid dynamics.

(ref: experiment written above, which showed special fluid dynamic of spiral and circulating movement in limited space by outer border of globe pattern.)

2-2. Cosmology from the point of view of Mam-factor hypothesis

Nowadays the explosion theory that a black hole might be a chance to form universe is believable to the most people. But they don't explain the origin of the black hole. In order to understand the formation of this hole, I hope to propose my idea though I am not physicist. I dare say this mechanism of mam-factor could be called mechanism of quantum physics. This inter-spherical circulating hydrodynamic movement of mam-factor might have the transferring capacity of changing pure factors into the factors with electro-magnetic power when they formed cluster.

If we suppose that the fine structure of the mam-factor existed in the universe, they might fill up the whole universe, and they might be origin of movement, the origin of forming black holes and big bangs, they might be the origin of alternation, and the origin of all existence. Finally they might be called "God", as a being of the invisible spirit of the mam-factor, the greatest energy of power, and the truth of nothing of no return as Suwoon said. If look from this point of view, there is no particles, and substances in the world that doesn't have the mam-factor, which might be a electromagnetic mono-pole (having no pole but a very easily changing specificity of electro-magnetic characters) because they would be the purest factor enough to be easily charged according to some change of the surrounding enviroment.

By some mechanism, mam-factor would form a very fine cluster, and then the cluster would have an opposite charge to the charge of original causative energy. A part of them could come to be gathered and formed a larger moving stream of cluster called an electron(electrove) among mam-factors being limited by the electromagnetic layer of the border from the mam-factor's sea of the cosmos. As I showed above, in this view point, the electron should not be particle but coincide and compound waves of mam-factors having character of distributing, separating to each wave or each factor again by some changing energy, and than they become stable state losing negative charge of itself. In this electromagnetic process would be recognized as the alternation process of energy which might be produced in the cosmos as well. Finally, on having negative charge, these energy appearance could be recognized as a phenomenon of overlaping waves as the big overlapped water waves appear in the stream of water, and so the movement style of electron in quantum theory could be made by the stream of mam-factor like a overlapped water waves flowing in the brook stream. And so the electrove(electron) might be circulating energy of the complexed mam-factor's cluster forming spiral wave in outer border of atom which formed by nucleon's gravity. And on the phenomenon of depriving energy, the overlapped mam-factor's waves in the state of having energy, might become again scattered to each mam-factor, to the flow of main stream of mam-factors. If expending such idea to the universe, the mam-factor being full in the universe, could make limited stream locally, and make movement of quantum theory by a certain mechanism [gathering phenomenon by electromagnetic power], and if they form some size of cluster[always moving] there might form larger circulation movement to create acceleration pulling mam-factors [in physics, the acceleration due to gravity known only, but I think another acceleration due to electromagnetic power, could be found. (eg: we can find that the electromagnetic power of iron particles moving near to the magnet becomes stronger and faster proportionally.).

If the clusters could form spiral circulating movement(composed of mam-factor, like electronic state) like tornado by some causative force complexed of gravity, positional energy, electro-magnetic power, and differentiations of temperature, it might be getting bigger and faster for being no resistance in the space.

At this time, they might be thought like a giant thread form, and than it might become pipe pattern containing inner space formed by the increasing velocity and volume of mam-factor's layer, accodingly the pipe pattern would become bigger and bigger having great negative pressure of the central space. The character of this stage, we can suggest that it might have some specificity in physics, according to the outer diameter becoming bigger, the negative pressure of the central space will increase, at last they could made the central space near to the absolute vacuum state. If this great absolute vacuum space formed in the universe, it might be a greatest vacuum hole in the universe. At last, the vacuum state of central part of the long tunnel, might become the absolute vacuum state. [let's call this state Absolute Vacuum State: AVS]. This AVS, with strong spiral circulation power of electromagnetic field which formed of mam-factors, could absorb not only all, the near materials, but mam-factors in certain limited area. So all beings pulled into the absolute vacuum space might become shrink to the smallest size because all of their fluid components will leak out by the strongest power of AVS caused by the greatest spiral circulation power of outer layer of finest mam-factor like the greatest tornado which has never seen on the earth. At the time of AVS, we can persue that the inner temperature of vacuum space will be decreased to the lowest temperature by the greatest absorption power of utmost vacuum state, and the inner components absorbed must shrink, and become to very hot state more and more with the concentrating fever. In this state, the materials might be the magma state with the naked nucleons and naked particles, which might be produced of gathered mam-factor by absorption power of AVS. At this time, the inner magma materials should have circulated by the greatest power of outer layer's spiral counterclockwise movement, and the outer space of mam-factor's layer become the state of magnetized with the both poles of long tunnel, which is produced by the rotating central magma. By this phenomenon, the both side of tunnel would form polarity, and there might be greatest magnetic field in the greatest universe, and than the greatest mam-factor's electromagnetic field would appear from one pole to the other, and than according to enlarging tunnel formed of mam-factor, the central vacuum space might become enlarged, so it would be said that this phenomenon could be the origin of endless enlargement of the universe. But this image of 'endless enlargement of universe' is not acceptable to the mam-factor hypothesis, because, as I wrote above, the greatest universe would be thought the greatest electro-magnetic field with the greatest vacuum tunnel through the central axial space connected one pole to opposite pole with the pattern of central vacuum space, just like rugby ball image with central longitudinal tunnel.

And for flexibility character of the outer wall formed of mam-factor, the vacuum center space could become larger more and more. [in this stage, the vacuum space might become the lowest temperature, because all the energy must be took out by the absortion power strengthened by the great rotating power of mam-factor's layer wall of cosmic size having great electromagnetic power]. I think this might be mechanism of black hole. Thus the material in AVS being compressed and stored with shrunk state, could get the highest temperature of condensation heat of itself, according to the increasing temperature, it might become the explosive state at last, and on becoming over limit of the condensing power, it must explode with the greatest scale in the universe, they would say this might be Big-Bang, the great explosion of shrunk materials in black hole. In physics, this explosion of black hole might be a chance to produce new universes and galaxies, the theory of beginning momentum of universe might be reasonable with this hypothesis.

By this Big-Bang, the first cosmos might had been broken, and debris of cosmos with vacuum tunnels might had scattered around the first cosmos. After first Big-Bang, I guess there might be great and partial Big-Bangs in each debris of universe, in which the same mechanism forming vacuum space might have been formed contineously. If say again, the explosions could break the central vacuum tunnels of the universes, and these tunnels broken by Big-Bangs could reform other universes, and these greater universes and small universes could appear, and thus so many universes and galaxies in the grand universe could be created. If we figure these relations of a part of universes, it might look like the upper portion of apple tree, having branches of tunnels, and apples of galaxies and universis. This idea of several Big-Bang have been occurred contineously, originated from the idea that the first Big-Bang might be smaller than the next, because the universe, formed with the outer layer of mam-fator's, which would have become larger and larger space with the elecric magnetic character, according to increasing account and enlarging amount of mam-factors. The separated partial cosmos and galaxies could exist by the partial mam-factor's stream layers, separated from the main greatest original cosmic stream of mam-factor. The hypothesis about many stages creation of Cosmos written above, is different from the hypothesis of one stage creation of Comos as most men and physicists have thought so far. If we think the first origin of the Cosmos, generally they said that a particle theory that cosmos formed from a big explosion of a finest particle without space. But if we think with my hypothesis, the first origin might be a Mam-factor's appearance, which had auto-division ability in the vacuum space. The former belongs to the material origin but the later belongs to the spirit origin. If the former might be truth, the scientists who have claimed the particle theory, must answer to the questions written below. Where the biggest energy of the original particle came from and how the whole materials in cosmos were created only with the one finest particle. And if the former had happened, it must appear again after that time, because the repetition and the duplication is the natural law of the formation and the alternation of the universe. If we think insight these natural specificity, we can assume that a certain phenomenon which can not be found again, it might be only the image which was created by our brain. To tell the truth, if not these spcificity of nature, none was created.

Here, I will show the interesting machine used in Korea for making pop-corn, with the explosive mechanism of the hot materials being under the high pressure. The operator insert dried corns to the central bulb portion of this machine made of iron mold, after locking the cap tightly with instrument, and heating the central bulb portion with petroleum gas flame on rotating the handle by hand or small motor. And it become high temperature, and high pressure that inner space bulb containing corn grains. After about 10 minutes it become reached to the proper pressure which the operator need (about 1 Mga: Mega pascal), and then he stop heating the machine and fix it to puff out inner materials into the net vessel like a fishing net. When handler open the cap with the portable lever, we can hear the big sound of explosion, with steam puffing out. The puffed out corns called twibab in Korea are very different from pop corn in Western in shape, they are changed to enlarged volume by 4 to 6 times, and to round ball shape when we compare with original corn seeds.

As the fact written above, a sudden explosion changed the soft materials heated, being inner space of limited form, to numerous materials which have round globe shape, through the process of sudden decreasing pressure. We have had physical knowledge that the natural law is the same in spite of their different size of alteration. If we explore with this truth, we can suppose that the reason why all the planets are showed globe pattern. So I dare think the origin of spiral movement of universe, and the origin of galaxies and planets might be the "Big-Bang" phenomenon which is formed in the utmost vacuum and cold space that is made by spiral circulating power of the greatest cosmic layer of mam-factor which have the greatest electromagnetic power.

1   2   3   4   5

2-3. In the point of view of recent philosophy

In western philosophy, the abstractive concept of God was identified in the era of Spinoza and Hegel, but by the empiricists Descartes and Kant this identity of God had not been accepted. At last, the great German philosopher I. Kant, was insisted that the pure reason of man which is very similar concept of the spirit in our mind.

He was the first philosopher in Europe to search for God as the 'pure reason' as a specificity of God in our mind, and his ethics showed in the article of the 'critique of pure reason' was a revolutionary idea and the highest value of virtue in his era. His idea of "categorical imperatives" might be a result of the ultimate moral state of the reason of mankind without the reality of God. Here we must not forget Nietzsche, another genius philosopher of German who had hoisted his new intuitionism flag on the desolate hill surrounded by Catholicism, unfortunaly having the wrong image of crazy man. And recently in the field of philosophy in America, Husserl and White Head had laid out a new logical basis for the reality of God. Through the history of above, all philosophical ideas have come down to near era, but it have been very hard to understand the reality of God. And at last to the mankind, new identity of God, which have the possibility of understanding the reality with physical hypothesis of this book based on the word of huryung-changchang*(ref: key word), which said by Suwoon in Korea, as Jesus in Israel. Accordingly, if this hypothesis is real, we might have to change our idea differentiated to the both parts of theological logics and physics, to one logics of physical theology, in future. And it will need for us to change our recognition to the new theory of 'equality of mam-factor and God' as below.

Exploration of equality

1) Certainty of recognition of equality

A. Certainty by scientific methodology
B. Certainty by metaphysical logics

2) Exploration with upper two methodologies.

i) Sentences about spirit
   a. Spirit is our heart. ---B
   b. We can commune with animals and plants with heart, ---A
   c. So all lives have spirit.---A, B

ii) Sentences about life
   a. Life originated from the super micro-particles like DNA. ---A
   b. There is substance which has both character of material specificity and life specificity in common like virus. ---A
   c. So there is possibility of ultimate fine being's existence with both specificity of life and material in cosmos.---A(though mam-factor's hypothesis)

iii) Sentences for conclusion
   a. That ultimate fine being can pass through finest structure of material and lives like atom. ---A
   b. That ultimate fine being can influence to our heart.---A
   c. We can call this being to be God.---A, B

3

New ecological and moral highway to 'the Idea' on the earth

-Donghak: Towards life and spirituality [5] by Choonsung Kim [6]

Abstract

This paper discusses Donghak, the first native religion in Korea, comprising a doctrine that pursues an ecocentered life and human spirituality. In the middle of nineteenth century, Donghak proclaimed human civilization as diseased the "Beginning of a New World." Donghak claims all human beings to be dignified beings that bear Hanullim (God, the ultimate reality) within. Hence Donghak teaches its adherents to "respect human beings as one would respect God [Hanullim]," on the promise that all creations of nature demand respect as a manifestation of God [Hanullim].

Donghak endeavors to recover human spirituality and provide humanity with new level of existence, or a living consciousness enjoined with the wider

---

[5]   Korea Journal, vol.42 No.4 Winter 2002, Reshaping Korean Philosophy for the Postmodern Era. Korean National Commission for UNESCO,

[6]   Kim, Choon Sung Ph.D: A professor in the Deparment of Liveral Arts, Arts College in Pusan, and the Dean of Donghak religional Institute. Her work predominantly focuses on the subject of the philosophy of Donghak. She, who had the amazing experiences to commune with holy spirit of Hanullim(God), has published a number of articles including, "The Contemporary Meaning of Haewol's Thought"(1999), "The Study of Nature and Ecocentric Life in Donghak"(2000), and "A Philosophical Approach to Yongdamyusa"(2001), e-mail: hwdang@hanmail.net

universe, by fostering communication with the reality of universal life. Donghak not only provides instruction about an ecocentered life, but also fosters the practice of it.

In this paper, I examine whether these ideas derived from Donghak are new and promising, and whether they can replace existing understandings of the world and our spirituality.

Introduction

Environmental pollution and the destruction of the ecosystem foretell the demise of all living things. Decertification is progressing at an alarmingly rapid speed in many parts of the world and meteorological disasters such as floods, typhoons, extreme heat waves and cold spells have killed numerous people and other living creatures. If climatic change continues to worsen in the future, survival on earth will become exceptionally difficult. In the face of this criticism, doubt is increasingly arising to scorn Western civilization, the pioneer of modernity.

Indian eco-feminist and environmental activist, Vandana Shiva, is critical of the gross destruction of life initiated by Western civilization in the name of progress, led by science and development projects which do not include any evaluation of the rapid speed of the disappearance of a variety of the life forms of our planet. She asserts that science and development do not belong to any universal category of progress, but rather are a specific design of Western patriarchy.[7] With a particular focus on modern science and crisis experienced in many ecosystem, she sternly sends the warning that if the world, especially our world view and life style, are not constructed anew, the existence of human beings will it self be threatened.[8]

It must be recognized that the problems currently experienced by humanity are not limited to certain areas or regions, but are global and general, and that it is imperative that we search for a new alternative for the sake of all humanity, nature, and human society as a single organic living entity, and the value of

---

[7]   Vandana Shiva, Saranamgi, trans. Kang, Su-young(Seoul Sol Publishing co., 1998); originally published as Staying Alive: Women Ecology Development in India.

[8]   Ibid, p.82.

treating each of this components as parts of single body in the creation of a new mode of life in coexistence. The patriarchal industrial culture of the Western world which sprouts scientific technology has dominated, conquered exploited the relatively weak. This has dichotomized all living things and understood them in conflictual and competitive relations. This perspective has overlooked precious spiritual values, which cannot be reduced to material values and has continued to destroy nature and kill life in the name of development and progress. Consequently, Western, male-centered ideologies are now rejected in many parts of the world and new discourses have immerged to establish a new value system and seek alternative. As the sense of crisis surrounding environmental problems intensifies, catch cries like "Save the Dying earth!" have become familiar. However, despite heightened interest in the environment, environmental problems are regarded as technological and economic issues. Many people believe that current environmental problems can be solved through further advancements in science an increase in the allocation of government funding. This indicates a disinterest in the fundamental problem and simply resorts to scientism to avoid this. Whitehead explains that "Of course most men of science, and many philosophers, use the positivistic doctrine to avoid the necessity of considering perplexing fundamental questions-in short, to avoid metaphysics and then save the importance of science by an implicit recurrence to their metaphysical persuasion that past does in fact condition the future.[9]

He also criticizes scienticism as nothing but a blind form of metaphysics.

Environmental destruction can not be solved simply through technology or money. This paper emphasizes the source of environmental problems to be as fundamental as our perspective of nature and the value of life. The question of the determination of our life values and attitudes is crucial. The environmental movement requires a more fundamental approach in addition to concrete practices to deal with our immediate problems. Here, by "fundamental approach," I mean a critical modification in our ways of thinking and living.

The new science emerging in the West urges such a fundamental change in our view of the earth, arguing that the earth is "Gaia," a gigantic body of life itself where all forms of life are connected in an intricate web. This

---

[9]   Alfred Whitehead, Gwannyum-ui moheom, trans. O Yuong-hwan (Seoul Hangilsa Publishing co., 1997) p. 214; Originally published as Adventures of Ideas.

organic world view demands a shift our understandings of the earth, from simply the "environment" humans live in, to an ecological understanding that acknowledges it is community shared by all living creatures. During this extraordinary period of cultural and social transition, the world has began to pay attention to the value of life in terms of "coexistence," "symbiosis" "and communal life," and there has been a surge of interest in spirituality and spiritual lifestyles that foster a connection with the essence of life. This interest in spirituality and human nature as the foundation of life has led to an increased interest in the religions of East. Interestingly, the achievements of modern physics have much in common with Eastern philosophical thought. As a relationship of mutual inspiration and wisdom develops between Western science, which investigates the objective world and Eastern wisdom, which pursues subjective enlightenment, intellectuals world wide have begun to reconsider intuition, insight and enlightenment, which were previously disregarded as mystical by the dominant rationalist ideology. This change is transforming our understanding of humanity and the world. It is now imperative that we adopt a new framework for our lives, and seek out the required new world view to generate a new way of life. As the science and religion of the West conquered the nations of the East through war, Choe, Jaewoo (pen name: Suwoon, 1824-1864), a Korean Confucian scholar, had spent many years in anguish searching for a new pattern of life. At last Suwoon could get his own answer on 5 April 1860.

The founder of Donghak [East Learning] in the mid-nineteenth century, Suwoon declared human civilization outdated and sick[10] and proclaimed all human beings to be worthy of respect as vessels containing the sacred Hanullim[11] [God, the ultimate reality] within. Through the employment of the concepts of sicheonju [all human beings and living things in our universe bear God within] and honwonilgi [a sacred energy that works in various on

---

[10]   The twelve imperial nations are suffering from plague. Is it not time for a new beginning? "Ansimga[song of comfort], in Yongdamyusa [Memorial songs of Yongdam]

[11]   In Donghak, the term Hanullim means the absolute, ultimate reality, very similar to the image of God, Choe, Jaewoo, the founder of Donghak, also called this cheon-ju in the scripture which he wrote in Chinese letter.

a variety levels], he maintained the existence of a sacred spirit that connects each individual with Hanullim with nature, with other human beings and even with entire universe. In other words, Suwoon offered a new paradigm of civilization with which to overcome the anthropocentric world view of the modern Western world.

He spoke of gaebyok [the beginning of a new world] to usher in a new civilization and construction a different framework for human life. The extensive meaning of the term gaebyok cannot be discussed in minute in detail. But I will focus on illuminating the implication of Donghak as an alternative world view through which to overcome the limitations of modern Western civilization and examine its potential to assist in our preparations for the future.

3-1. Gaebyok: A New Way of Life

Suwoon established Donghak on 5 April 1860 based on his personal religions experience.[12] What is the nature of this newly created religion? Suwoon opened up an entirely new horizon of idea for Hanullim [God], the universe and human beings. He claimed that human beings have an inseparably close inner relationship with God and they are cosmic being in that they are connected with all other beings in the universe through connecting energy [gihwa]. Human consciousness of these inner and outer relationships will result in the establishment of a new world [gaebyok] within the dimension of human reality. If such enlightened human beings form a community, this becomes the beginning of a new level of civilization. Let us examine what he meant by the beginning of a new level of civilization within the dimension of human reality, considered a state in which humans bear God within them and breathe in conjunction with the universe. Through a deeply religious meditation practice, which is often called the meditation of "Osim jeuk yeosim [My mind is your mind]"-Suwoon had listened this sentence via his amazing experience from which he realized that the mind of Hanullim[God] and his own were not two but one.[13] He also learned that a great sacred energy forms

---

[12]　Suwoon described this experience in detail in "Podeogkga[poems on spreading virtue] and "Nonhagmun"[Discussion on Doctrine].

[13]　In Nonhakmun, Hanullim said to Suwoon that "my mind is your mind."

in each human being and in all the creatures in the universe, and that this energy serves to intervene, order and unify all living things. Thus, he declared all people to be equal and worthy of respect, and considered all things as sacred for they all carry Hanullim within them. Suwoon taught that it is pointless to try to find Hanullim outside of one.[14] By realizing the concept of sicheonju, he did not separate Hanullim from human beings and tried to understand human life at the level of the universe as a whole. Choe Si-hyeong(pen name Haewol, 1827-1898), was ordained by Suwoon as the Second Great Master of Donghak, and inherited this organic view of humanity and nature, consistently advocating that all things in the universe are connected through a sacred energy and continuously evolving from the action of life engaged in continuous interaction. In a further step, he elevated all beings to a position of reverence. The following citation from Haewol's teachings demonstrates the penetration of the great energy into each and everything in the universe and his personal practice of the truth in his life.

> I have always said that all things and events are a manifestation of Hanullim [God]. If you agree with this, you must also agree that is not a thing which Hanullim does not eat and which Hanullim does not be eaten by. This sounds absurd, but if think twice, we could know it might be a reason for the biased view of the human mind. What would it be like if things were seen from Hanullim's point of view? To bring about the connection of sacred energy, Hanullim has those homogeneous to mutually help one another and has those heterogeneous ones eat Hanullim so that their spirit can be connected. Therefore, Hanullim cultivates species through homogenous linkage on the one hand while promoting growth and development of different species through the relationships between the heterogeneous on the other. In short, that Hanullim both eat and be eaten can be understood as the Idea of Hanullim's putting into action the connecting sacred energy. When the Great Devine Master Suwoon explicated on the meaning of si[to bear], he stated that naeyusillyeong [the internal divine spirit] meant Hanullim and oeyugihwa [the external connection of sacred energy] implies that

---

[14]   "Believe in Hanullim[God] not me, don't search for Hanullim far away, Hanullim is within you." Gyohunga[poem of instruction]

Hanullim both eat and be eaten. The marvelous law of heaven and earth be connected through this sacred energy.[15]

Based on the conceptualization of the entire universe as connected through a sacred energy, Haewol explained the relationship among things in the universe through the concept of icheon-sikcheon [Hanullim eat Hanullim: God eat God / Hanullim breed Hanullim, God breed God].

This doctrine is a very interesting and unfathomable, this idea that Hanullim be an eater at the same time be the eaten reveals that the entire universe is conceived as a network of mutual dependent relationship of alteration. Of course, as Haewol said, this is so in Haullim's point of view.

To understand this doctrine, let's think about human beings, we eat vegetables, rice, meat and milk so on, but all that is grown with the organic or inorganic energy source created naturally, which is belonging to Hanullim [God]. So humans, as the most out standing spiritual energy entity eat the essential energy of the universe. Because all sacred energy is really the one energy of Hanullim, as Haewol states, it can be said that Hanullim eat Hanullim. It is easy to understand this idea to think food chain in biology. The doctrine of sicheonju, which Donghak offers as a new paradigm, presents life on a new, cosmic dimension in which human beings can recover and revere their sacredness, and in turn respond and communicate with the all in the heaven and on the earth. This new paradigm connects nature with actual human life and discovers the sacredness within it, elevating it to an object of reverence. Furthermore, it entails contemporary ecological thinking by understanding nature and the phases of our lives, within this connective framework, and by seeking a life of aesthetic harmony between the body and the mind.

As the new paradigm, sicheonju can generate "another new beginning" for human civilization and the principle foundation of the new beginning sought by Donghak adherents. In Donghak, a new beginning is not brought about suddenly nor made by an absolute supernatural being, but by those human beings who transform themselves through internal spiritual change and construct a new world. Human being creator of a new life for humanity, in a holistic way inclusive of politics, economics, society and culture, achieve harmony among humans, human to nature, and human to the universe.

---

[15]   Hanullim feed on Hanullim, In Sermons of Haewol, the Scripture of Donghak

Thus Donghak has focused on the "here and now," "this world" and "the life of humans" on earth rather than emphasizing any other abstract, transcendental values disengaged from live reality. Since its inception, Donghak followers have not turned from contemporary social problems, such as support for the nation, and comfort for other people despite of many attempts of persecution and suppression. For instance, Donghak members have always been in the vanguard of movements to protest corrupt officials of the late dynasty, called the Donghak revolution, and the New Culture Movement in Gapjin year and March 1st Independent Movement against the Jap. ruler in 1919 in our history. Thus Donghak devotees have had the greater ambition and great pain for new beginning of human civilization. Donghak's philosophy has opened a new horizon in understanding of humanity to all human beings as the unifier of Hanullim[God], an abstract metaphysical being, and the universe, the concrete world of nature and all things contained within.

It is not an ideology but a concrete historical reality in Korea in modern history that human who gave a concrete form to a metaphysical ideal existence called Hanullim to be realized in the real world.

Donghak declared there to be a new dimension to life and a possibility of the new beginning of an old civilization through the epistemological shift incited by the doctrine of sicheonju. This fosters the capacity to intensely feel life and the spirit of the universe acting through one's body and mind, and encourages the act of "revering" them as one would one's parent, and finally to engage in the public realm of wider society in this way. Donghak urges one to cultivate the true self by realizing one's innate sacredness and eternal life and to create a new civilization in which such actors establish true equality through reverence and "bearing." In this way, the new beginning does not remain at the level of individual character, but is treated at the level of civilization.

3-2. Gihwa: An Ecologically Aware Being

The modern civilization of the West is based on dualism and on mechanical view of the world, which focuses on the relationships between the mental and physical, and between humanity and nature as oppositional. Communal values and living practices once engaged among humans, between human and society, and human beings and nature have been disbanded and the relationship between human and all other living forms faces a serious crisis due to the destruction of the ecosystem. Members of Eastern societies have long sought harmony with nature, by maintaining a monistic tradition and an organic world view. In the eastern traditions, nature is considered the origin of life and the manifestation of an abundant flow of spiritual energy. Thus in Eastern philosophies, nature is a treasure house and the origin of life at the same time. The order and cycles of change within nature are unspoken lessons and wisdom given to humans.

In the East, nature is not perceived as a material object, much less an object of conquest and exploitation[16] nor regarded as a physical object of modern science, but rather as a living realm which never ceases to create, and the foundation of the whole living world in which one concretely live one's life. Most Eastern philosophers have believed that the universe is full of energy from time immemorial. They have held an organic world view in which the world is perceived as dimensions of singular energy. Moreover, they endeavor to explain the universe through the concept of samjae[three elements composing the universe, heaven, earth and human], ohaeng[five standard symbols of the alteration of the energy in universe; water, tree, fire, soil and metal; there are also three directions between each step: positive, negative and neutral] and yin and yang[plus and minus; two basic factors of energetic change and movement]. Inheriting this concept of three elements with five steps of alternation and two factors, Donghak presents an organic view of heaven, earth and humanity and explains the universe as the action of one great energy. Suwoon said that "Heaven is the center of ohaeng: earth is the foundation of ohaeng; and human being is supreme spiritual manifestation of ohaeng. This idea is very important to mankind, because this appears different from the Confucian's outlook in the point not to be regarded heaven and earth

---

[16]   Haewol said, "Heaven and earth are our parents, and parents are heaven and earth. Thus heaven and earth are one with parents. the womb of mother is the womb of heaven and earth. People know the womb of parents, but do not know that of heaven and earth. Heaven covers and earth houses us, what is this but grace? The sun and the moon shed light on us. What is this if not a blessing? All things in the universe are born from harmony. What is this if not the creation of the truth and the spirit of heaven and earth? "He also taught, "To revere Hanullim and serve Hanullim [God] like ones parents are one's duty as human being."

simply as the order of energy system of ohaeng,[17] but as a totality of the spirits, yin-yang, and nature(harmony among the spirits and the forces of yin-yang). Suwoon scorned the shamanic worship, saying "If they do not know heaven and earth is the spirit and the spirit is yin-yang, what is the use of studying the scriptures?[18] To Suwoon, spirit is real, it is the activity of energy of heaven and earth, thus it simply become yinyang.

Suwoon's argument is that the metaphysical truth, the human heart/soul, and the natural orders are connected as one. The natural order is sign of Hanullim [God]'s work. From time immemorial, spring and fall come alternately and the alternation of the four seasons never breaks in its order. And this is a clear sign of Hanullim [God]'s work manifested in the world.[19] Donghak subsumes this traditional Eastern view of nature and at the same time considered the world as one of "harmony" which the great sacred energy of Hanullim [God] is continuously creating and changing. Therefore, nature is not just material or energetic, but an embodiment of the holy, formless God. While Western modernity makes a clear distinction between the divine and the natural order, Donghak foresees the dawn of a new civilization by opening the blocked channels of communication existing between three [heaven, earth and human] and reconnecting them. Through the concept of "bearing" Suwoon establishes a superb linkage between internal relatedness to God and the external interactivity in operation among all things in the universe. Donghak differs little from other qi-philosophies in the sense that it claims the universe to be filled with one cosmic energy. However, Donghak emphasizes the spiritual nature of the movement of this energy, through acts such as intervention and order.

While other qi-philosophies view humans nature as an integrated framework and attempt to discover common laws through which one can live a healthy and an aesthetic life, Donghak pursues such a life through the subjective cultivation of the mind.

Qi-philosophies focus on humans' passive nature and its conformity with universal energy, whereas the concept of energy in Donghak emphasizes the active nature of the human mind/soul.

---

[17]   "On learning Truth," in Eastern Great scripture written by Suwoon.
[18]   "Podeokga"[Poem of Morality], in Memorial poems of Yongdam.
[19]   "On spreading virtue," in Eastern Great Scripture.

As this active nature of the mind/ soul of humanity have its roots in Hanullim [God], the energy is ultimately connected to Hanullim. Suwoon's understanding of God becomes significant at this point.

Suwoon does not conceptualize "Hanullim [God]" distinctly; instead, he explains its meaning and mode of existence through the concept of "si [bearing]."[20]

He says, "The word si means one existing internally as a sacred mind / soul and externally as an active energy connected to it. All understand and do not move from it. "Here, naeyusillryung [the internal sacred spirit] and oeyugihwa[the external connecting energy] is the way that Hanullim[God] exists in all creation. That is, everything in the universe, including humans, has an innate sacred spirit and an external sacred connecting energy. When the internal sacred spirit and external energy come together and form a body, a life is born. Thus, deep inside this life exists a sacred spirit and a single sacred energy. Becoming one with this deep sacred spirit and the universal energy and not separating the two is what Suwoon means by the expression gakjiburi [to attain complete enlightenment and not part from it.] While the internal sacred spirit and the external connecting energy refer to the mode of Hanullim's[God's] existence, gakjiburi is the human realization of consciousness and practice of the mode of life existence, too. Therefore, in Donghak Hanullim [God] is not an absolute transcendental universal being. In Suwoon's view it is the ultimate reality that one sacred energy creates all things in the universe and communicates with them ceaselessly as an internal sacred being and external connecting energy. Thus, God [Hanullim] is not a metaphysical real being, but "a being" in the process of becoming or in progress.

Concerning ju [lord or sir], he also said that "We must revere Hanullim [God] as one reveres one's parents."[21] This means that Hanullim work concretely to create everything in the universe, including humans, and take care of them, just as our parents do for us. Because humans and all other creatures are born through this great energy and live independently within this great energy, Hanullim is addressed by an honorific term with the same Korean differential suffix, "-nim or -lim," used when addressing parents. An examination of the principle doctrines of Donghak showed that Hanullim

---

[20] On learning Truth, in Eastern Great Scripture
[21] On learning Truth, in Eastern Great Scripture

[God], humans and all other creatures are inseparable and they are one in origin. Moreover, creatures and nature are not mere materials; they are an embodiment of the sacred infinite Hanullim and a concrete form of the formless God. Haewol extends the concept of sicheonju to all creatures and make it even more.

> We, humans, are born bearing the sacred spirit of Hanullim and live on with Hanullim's sacred spirit in us. But how can we say that human alone bear Hanullim [God]? There is not a thing in the universe which does not bear Hanullim [God]. The bird's chirping is also Hanullim's voice. Every life is born only after it receives this mind and energy. All the creation in the universe is penetrated by the same energy and mind.[22]

Asserting that it is not humans alone that bear Hanullim[God], but that animals, plants and even lifeless things bear Hanullim, Haewol urges us to realize this and practice it in every day life, i.e., live the life of "bearing Hanullim[God]."

Hanullim is alive in everyday life. Rather, life itself is a self-expression of God. One who knows this as a fact bears Hanullim, but one who does not know this does not bear Hanullim. In Donghak, the life of bearing [si] Hanullim [God] means living with the same energy and mind that penetrates everything in the universe. Those who live a life of bearing cannot think of nature as an object to conquer, neighbors as foes to compete with and to beat, animals and plants as prey or a simple material mass. Therefore, there would be no killing even if it were not forbidden.

> There is not a single thing that does not bear Hanullim[God]. If people realize this there will be no killing even if it is not forbidden. A phoenix flies in where sparrow eggs are not broken. Forests grow thick if tree buds are not picked. Each of the 3,000 animals has a species to breed and each of the 3,000 hairy insects have a life to live. Respect everything, then virtue will spread afar.[23]

---

[22]   Invocations to the Sacred Spirit, Sermons by Divine Teacher Haewol

[23]   How to treat Humans and things: Sermons by Divine Teacher Haewol,

The Donghak religious philosophy differs from the dichotomous thinking and dualism of the West that distinguishes the body from phenomena, matter from mind, God from humanity, humanity from nature, and God from nature, in the endeavor to understand them as separate entities. God, humans and all other creatures in the universe are different expressions and outcomes of the activities of jigi[the ultimate energy]. In this sense, Donghak can be classified as a variant of monism. Claiming God, humanity and nature are one in origin; Donghak fosters a new understanding of nature. Since Descartes, Western dualism has seen nature as nothing more than the surroundings, the environment or resources', producing a world view in which nature is an object to be dominated or exploited by human beings. But in the notion of sicheonju[bearing Hanullim;God], nature is no longer perceived as the environment of resources, but as an embodiment of Hanullim or Hanullim's body. Haewol concretize this notion in his idea of "Samgyeong[Honoring of the Three]."

> Firstly, humans must honor Hanullim [God]. This is the first principle of the Way expounded by the late Great Teacher Haewol. One who does not know why one must honor Hanullim does not know how to love the truth. This is because Hanullim [God] is at the center of the truth. Honoring Hanullim does not mean honoring a higher being in an empty space. Honoring one's own mind is the right way of honoring Hanullim.
>
> Secondly, honor fellow human beings. Honoring Hanullim comes in effect through honoring human beings. If one honors Hanullim but not one's fellow human beings, it is the same as knowing the principles of farming but but not sowing the seeds. If one abandons humans and venerates only Hanullim, it is the same as dumping out water needed to be relieved from a drought. Thirdly, honor things. One cannot reach the highest stage of virtue by only honoring human beings. One can unite with the virtue of connecting with heaven and the earth only by honoring things.[24]

---

[24]   Samgyeong[Honoring the Three], in Sermons by Divine Teacher Haewol.

This is completely different from the conventional Western view of nature based on a reason-centered view of humanity and a dualistic notion of the material and the spiritual, which have made the reckless violation of nature possible. Indeed, we can not unite with the spirit of heaven and earth unless we reach a state revering all creatures. If this is done, the crisis of ecosystem and modern civilization can be overcome. Reverence for heaven is common in most religions and thus is known to all. Meanwhile, reverence for human kind has been acknowledged as the highest of all values since the birth of humanism. What is particularly interesting in Donghak is the reverence for things not found in the teachings of any other religious person or philosopher. This is an expression unique to Donghak. It teaches us to honor all things in nature as we do God or fellow human beings. In the west the modern era started with the awareness that human consciousness is different from that of things, and that humans exist independently without depending on an absolute God. Donghak does not deny this, but it does not stop at this. Because the sacred spirit of God penetrates everything in nature, one must learn to revere those things and only when this is done can one reach the highest level of morality. This does not mean a return to the time of animism, but an expansion and deepening of human consciousness. It means that humans must learn to see the divine in things, the sacred in fellow human beings, and infinity and eternity in God. It is not surprising that from the notion of reverence for things, Haewol developed the idea that heaven and earth are our parents.

> Heaven and earth are our parents and our parents are heaven and earth. Thus, heaven and earth are one with our parents. The womb of parents is the womb of heaven and earth. People know the logic of the womb of parents, but do not know that of heaven and earth. Milk is grain generated from the human body and grain is milk of heaven and earth. The womb of parents is the womb of heaven and earth. A child sucks milk from his mother's breasts, which is the milk of heaven and earth. When the child grows, he eats grain, which is the milk of heaven and earth.[25]

---

[25]   Heaven and earth are parents, Sermons by Divine Teacher Haewol.

Haewol claims that people know the logic of the womb of parents but do not know that of the bosom of heaven and earth, so they do not feel the need to serve and be dutiful to heaven and earth. By arguing that "grain is the milk of heaven and earth," he indicates that humans grow on grain or milk of heaven and earth as a child grows on mother's milk. Comparing Haewol's doctrine of filial piety with Confucius, which teaches for one to serve all creation in the universe as one's parents, Confucius' doctrine seems narrow in scope. Haewol believes that because one not only receives one's body from one's parents but also gains nutrients and energy from the products of the universe, one must show gratitude to them. To Haewol, heaven and earth are not only the base of our lives, but our parents who give birth to us and raise us, and who deserve our reverence. He treats nature as a sacred, holy life, or as God itself. Haewol lived out these beliefs by sanctifying this attitude in every day practice. A model of a sanctified life is revealed in his teaching "Treat land as dearly as your mother's fleshes." Here we meet the ideal of an ecologically aware lifestyle.

> The universe is filled with one cosmic energy, so one should not dare to take a careless step. I was resting when a child passed by me quickly wearing clogs. The click clack of a clogs reverberated through the earth. I stood up frightened and said smoothing my chest. "The sound of the child's clogs made my heart ache. Treat land as preciously as your mother's flesh."[26]

This experience was ultimately not a result of rational or philosophical thinking, but an awakening experience arising from a deep religious spirituality. This made it possible for Haewol to live it practically in real life. It is at these moments that human life is sublimated to the universal level. From his teaching to treat land as one's mother and to serve and be dutiful to it, one confirms that the essence of the new ethics needed today is "reverence."[27] Haewol's reverence is not limited to reverence for one's father or the king as in Confucianism, but extends to one's mother, wife and all living things, including nature.

Haewol's understanding of sicheonju[bearing Hanullim; God] which took root in his life through practice, serves as an illustration of human existence

---

[26] Sincerity, reverence and faith, Sermons by Divine Teacher Haewol.

[27] Busan Art College, ed. Haewol Choe, Sihyeong gwa Donghak Sasang

lived at a new dimension. In addition to the teachings above, he thought "If saliva or snivel is spattered on the land, wipe it off." and "Spitting afar, sniveling afar, or sprinkling water afar is the same as spitting on the face of your parents or heaven and earth, so please be careful." Though this may at first appear as an ethical percept of virtue, it is not something externally enforced, but a behavioral norm acquired from the existential experience of actually feeling pain in his heart when he failed to do it.

What should be noted here is that Haewol's understanding of heaven, earth and nature did not remain at the conceptual level, rather it was concretized and practical in real life. It was not simply an ecological concept, but a direct embodiment of an ecologically profound existence. He reached a state in which he actually felt the pain of heaven and earth. It surpassed the conceptual level of viewing nature as a transformed life through a reverent attitude. It does not stop at ecological awareness, but continues into living an ecological life. It means one's life is changed entirely and becomes sacred with complete realization that Hanullim [God] acts in the self as a divine spirit and outside the self as a connecting energy. One reaches the state where one can feel that heaven and earth are not separate from the self and have become one with the body. One is receptive to silent messages from heaven, earth and nature. Here the objective order of heaven and earth and the subjective experience of humans become one. Donghak pursues a harmonious life with heaven, earth and nature by seeking a fundamental transformation of body and mind. In this way, nature in Donghak is a living organism and a world filled with Hanullim's [God's] Ultimate Energy and Spiritual Energy, so it holds divinity or rather is divinity itself. Humans and all things depend on the connecting energy of heaven and earth for life, so they must revere heaven and earth like their own parents. The true nature of life cannot be understood by theory of knowledge, but reveals itself when felt through one's mind. Thus, Haewol teaches that one can truly practice the Way only if one reveres not only God and human being but things as well. Everyone with experience knows that reverence is not achieved through reason or logic. Reverence is based on not conflictual, but interdependent and equal relations.

Modern day catch phrases such as "Protect nature," "Save the environment," or "preserve the ecosystem" are based on a rational attitude and conflicting relations with nature and environment.

It is time for the environmental movement to go beyond its realistic and practical struggles and to try a more fundamental approach by presenting a new dimension of human life. What is needed is not just transformation through ecological awareness, but an ecological life.

It is high time for humanity to realize and increase the value of life. For this, one must be able to emphasize life. One can find the potential and wisdom to resolve the problems facing humanity in the life of Haewol, a hard-core ecologist who lived in complete harmony with all creations in the universe. Haewol's understanding of nature contains a new world view which embraces both creationist theology and evolutionary science and presents a Korean model to the recent achievement of new science at the juncture of a shift to a new paradigm.

3-3. Sillyeong[Divine Spirit]: Harmony between womanhood and manhood

These days spirituality is often discussed as an alternative to overcome the conflicts and contradictions of human society and to coexist in symbiosis with all living forms existing on the earth. David Steindler Rast claims that spirituality is the mode of existence where religious experience is manifested in or seeps into every day life.[28] Spirituality refers to a fusion between the mystical world and every day life, or sympathy with life in the universe. It can also mean the state of mind that fosters the ability to communicate and sympathize with the essence of existence. It is this intuition and insight that enables one to connect with the essence of things. It is the thing that is alive inside all things. And so, a spiritual life is a life in which one communicates with, feels, and responds to the inner essence of all things engaging in direct relations rather than a superficial, external relation. Spiritual life differs from rational life in which all things are objectified, analyzed and understood as objects. In the former, one does not distingish things from the self and feels the organic relationship with them in one's body and mind. Thus, spiritual life

---

[28] FRitjof Capra, et al., Sin-gwahak-gwa yeongseong-ui sidae, trns. Kim-jaehui: Pumyang co.,1999, p.33 original published as Belonging to the universe: Explorations on the Frontiers of Science and Spirituality.

deals with essence as well as relations, is unbiased and whole, and seeks life at a universal level. What does it mean exactly to say that humans are organically relate to the universe? Is it an ordinary state of mind, or a different state of mind free from ordinary life? In the east, what is ordinary and extraordinary at the same time is called Cheondo[Heavenly Way].

In a famous aphorism in the Daodejing that "Dao that can be expressed is not the eternal Dao." This sentence makes it clear that the Heavenly Way is beyond expression and human understanding. This is also the case in Confucianism. "In nature, the Heavenly Way is so profound and mysterious that human intellect can not grasp it". But the mysterious subtleties of the Heavenly Way begins to show through the sage's practice of virtue. The sage never explains the Heavenly Way in words; he just realizes it with pure virtuous acts." this means that the sage works the Heavenly Way in reality.[29] We can only conform the Heavenly Way in the sage. In Buddhism, this place is often conceptualized as Seong[nature] and is expressed as Gong[space], Mu[non being] or Heo[emptiness]. Some times, it is explained using such concepts as "neither existent nor non-existent," "neither impure nor pure" and "neither increasing nor decreasing." In the Bhagavad Gita, Krishna, who is regarded as an embodiment of the spirit of India and is worshiped as a living God there, proclaims, "There is no sun, no moon or no light. Once you get in there, You can never get out. That is the highest place I am."[30] That place can be called the essence of the center of existence. One cannot say that is exists or does not exist. In a Buddhist expression, it is the place which can neither be thought of nor not be thought of. Both being and non-being come from it. This is the place where being and non-being are together and which transcends them both at the same time. Thus it is impossible to explain what spirituality is. Krishna state the following about himself: "All things that exist are mortal and thing that do not change are immortal. But there is the highest being above them all. That is called Paramatma[the self on earth]. The immortal God enters Samgye[the three worlds] and supports them. I transcend the mortal and I am higher than the immotal. I am revered as Paramatma in this world and

---

29   Yang zuhan, Jungyongcheolhak[philosophy of the doctrine of the Mean], trans. Hwang gapyeon, Seogwangsa Publishing co., 1999, p.317
30   The Bhagavad Gita, annotated by Ham seokheon, Hangilsa bublishing co.,1996,

in the Vedas[knowledge]."[31] How, then, can one explain that place? This is why metaphors usually employed to describe the place. It can not be directly described, depicted or expressed.

One of the most common metaphors employed in Confucianism, Buddhism and Daoism is that of a mirror. A mirror reflects whatever is placed in front of it but it has no colors or shapes, and does not sway or move. Likewise, the place of the Heavenly Way is empty but active. So everyone is silent about this place. Laozi states, "One who knows [knower] does not speak." Buddha replied with silence when he was asked if God exists. Suwoon provided no interpretations of Heaven. Refusing to describe or interpret it, he explained the way as mu-geuk-dae-do[the Infinite Great Way] and as the non-distinction of bultaekseonak[no choice of good or evil]. The Infinite Great Way means the empty locus of origin and non-distinction between good and evil means the realm beyond relativity. Of course he was not completely silent about the center of the eternally tranquil internal mind. In explaining the meaning of bearing, he said that the divine spirit is inside. The divine spirit is Suwoon's way of expressing the ultimate being. Suwoon said that one could directly communicate with the divine spirit inside and that to live according to the place was to live bearing Hanullim[God], as stated above. Hanullim is true self and to live bearing Hanullim is "nothing other than the self becoming the self." A paradox is often used to explain what it is to live a life as the true I. This is common in traditional Eastern thought. A paradox can be very effective, from the idea that a divine sprit exists deep inside of life in the phenomenal world. The metaphor of mirror is a paradox, too. It is quite paradoxical that something completely tranquil and empty performs an action of reflecting everything. In the chapter titled "bulyeongiyeon[Not so, Yet so]" in Donggyeongdaejeon[Eastern Great scripture], Suwoon provided a logical explanation of spirituality, divine spirit, Haullum[God] and Heavenly Way. Based on keen observations of things and reflection on human affairs, he explains in "Not so, Yet so" that the phenomenal world which we can easily understand, listen and see can only exist in an inseparable relation to the world which we can not understand, listen or see.

Unlike modern philosophy which led to the flourishment of subjective philosophy in recognition of the constitutive ability of reason and active and directive consciousness, Donghak gives focus to receptive and non-directive

---

spirituality while being based on firmative power and directiveness. Often Western reason is called a masculine principle and Eastern spirituality is called a feminine pinciple. Even if one does not agree with it completely, it is true that modern Western philosophy gives an excessively superior status to rationality. The roots of the destruction of ecosystem, the conquest of other cultures and socio-political engineering can be traced to the constitutive and directive of Western philosophy. In the East, the formative directive quality of the mind is treated as a kind of desire or individual distortion. The true self reveals itself after proactive energies such as directiveness and constitutive ability completely decrease, and state or place is viewed as the truth. Suwoon explains that after this is reached, all actions are divested of intention, directiveness, constitutiveness and proactiveness, and the intention of heaven alone is realized. He also employs the concept of muwee iwha[becoming without acting] to describe the activities of mind after entering the place of tranquility. Laozi compares this place to a female, but this seems inappropriate from the perspective of Donghak. It would be more plausible if it is viewed as a place where yin and yang are joined and transcended. In Donghak, conflict between feminity and masculinity disappears with spirituality. However, because the locus of spirituality is in the mind, feminity and masculinity can not disappear at the level of the body. There can be no difference or discrimination between men and women as spiritual beings. Interpreting "ju" in the word si-cheon-ju in Nonhagmoon [main invocation in the chapter of On Learning Truth in the Eastern Great Scripture], Suwoon says that "One must revere Hanullim[God] as one's parent." Here he makes it clear that Hanullim[God] possesses not only masculinity but also feminity. That Hanullim[god] is not father but a parent means that God is always revealed as a union of feminity and masculinity in the phenomenal world. Indeed Suwoon takes up the problems of women first, after his religious experience in 1860. His ansimga[song of comfort which consists of elaborate caring entreaties to his wife to initiate the new beginning in the new era. After his enlightenment, he spread virtue to his wife Lady Park before anyone else and freed their two female servants. One of them became his daughter-in-law, and the other was adopted as his daughter, which was quite radical even by the standard of his time. He practiced gender equality in his life and worked toward harmony with his wife. Following his enlightenment, Suwoon wrote scriptures both in Chinese letters for Confucianists and in Hangle[Korean letter, King Saejong made] for the most of people[non-Chinese letter-educated] to spread his belief.

In "Song of Comfort", which he wrote for women, he called his wife "my venerable wife" or "my virtuous wife," expressing his utmost respect for her rather than his authority as a husband. He did not confine his wife to the private realm but treated her as a partner with whom to discuss social issues and national problem.[32] Sicheonju is a realization that humans are respectable being who have Hanullim[God] in themselves and a declaration of equality of humanity. The word means that man does not refer only to men but all human beings, including women.

Attaining profound religious spirituality from Suwoon's teachings, Haewol presents completely new, unconceivable at that time, views on women and children who were outsiders in the patriarchal Confucian society. Stating the "Woman is the master of the family" and Children have Hanullim[God] in themselves, so beating a child is the same as beating Hanullim[God]," he asserts a radically different conception of women and condemns repression and violence against powerless. Haewol does not merely call for the liberation of women: he seeks a rediscovery about women and a creation of "feminity" as the character of new civilization. For women to become true actor of new era, feminity, life-creating ability and spiritual sensitivity of women must be developed through divine spirituality.

The fact that Haewol's only writings are on women's prenatal culture and every day ethics demonstrates best the interest he had in feminity.

In "Naechik[Rules for Women]" and "Naesudomun[A Writing on the Cultivation of Women], he presents how women can attain spirituality in great detail. Naechik, a writing on prenatal culture, discusses guide line s for health and proper attitudes for women during pregnancy. On the surface, it does not seem very different from the teachings of prenatal training in the East. The critical difference is that it does not just offer tips on how to give birth to a good human being, but it presents principles of virtue on how to nurture Hanullim [God]. Haewol regards pregnancy as the advent of Hanullim, the energy of heaven and earth. To grow a baby's life in one's body is to directly experience Hanullim, Thus, prenatal culture or the process of

---

32 "It is in danger. It is really in danger. The fortune of our nation is in danger. Why has it become so bad? My noble wife, look currently and be at peace. My noble wife, do not panic or worry. Memorize these lyrics and sing the song of peace when spring comes."

nurturing Hanullim [God] becomes the most precious form of self-cultivation. Haewol earnestly entreats, "The ultimate truth of heaven and earth is in 'Rules for women' and 'Writing on the Cultivation of Women.' Please do not overlook them practice it as written." In "A Writing on the Cultivation of Women" he emphasizes that we must tell Hanullim[God] everything before acting. To tell everything in one's mind is an every day discipline to practice in real life the teaching that heaven and earth are one with our parents. This is the way to cultivate and protect one's mind and in and through every day life. Those two writings contain practical methods to attain a high level of mental cultivation or the core of refining one's body and mind in Donghak, which is often expressed as the state of susimjeonggi[keeping a good mind and having the right spiritual force]. In this teachings, Haewol opened the way for women to be treated like Hanullim[God] and to realize the truth by revering and serving Hanullim sincerely in every day life. Patriarchal male dominated culture makes abstract transcendental values centered on rationality absolute while destroying concrete vitality, a feminine principle, and feminity. The order of the universe, nature, life and human society are no exception. When we look at the concrete, real life of Haewol who declared that "The bird's chirping is also Hanullim's[God's] voice," we can tell that he felt, served and revered life of universe in his whole body. His teachings represent the spirit and life of the universe. In Donghak, probably the most representative example of spirituality expressed in everyday life is harmony between husband and wife. While in Confucianism is found a vertical family order such as hyo [filial piety], these is no horizontal family order like harmony between husband and wife. Haewol proclaims that husband and wife are not in a relationship of domination and subordination, but one of equal complementary in which both side strive to achieve harmony. For equal relations, women must be held with greater importance. He states, "Women were oppressed before, in the new era they will make many people live through their spiritual enlightenment. It is the same as the fact that all humans are born from a mother's womb and grow," predicting the birth of a new civilization. He forces the coming of new civilization based on feminity in the following passage:

> The woman is the master of the family. She prepares food, makes clothes, raises children, hosts guests and is in charge of the ancestral rites offerings. If she prepares food without sincerity, Hanullim will not respond. If she

raises children without care, they will not grow up honest, so the spiritual cultivation of a wife is the foundation of the Dao [Way] of our religion. From now on we have many spiritually enlightened women. I would say, nine females for every male.

Women were oppressed before, but in the new era they will save many people through their spiritual enlightenment. It is the same as all humans being born from a mother's womb and growing up.[33]

Haewol asserts the importance of the cultivation of women, who perform all the menial tasks but are not treated as valuable, by stating that they are masters of family and predict s that they will be the main actors in the new civilization. The new civilization will not require authoritative dominant power but try to realize the ability of life to "bear" and "make others live" in the holy life world by exercising their vital nature. Thus, gender equality does not mean women attacking the privileged males in a structure of conflict with them. The feminist movement must move beyond conflictual relations between men and women and consider men as partner to ally and unify with for common goals. He thinks that men and women are more than just partner; they can not exist independently of each other in any circumstances. Therefore, to be true leader in the new civilization, women must seek, instead of conflict and struggle with men, a transformation within and the cultivation of their life-creating ability and mental sensitivity trough the divine quality in them. Whether one is a man or a woman, one becomes a true human being when one reaches spirituality. To be a true human being means to live a harmonious life with one's spouse in actual life. Thus, Haewol states that "harmony between husband and wife is the end of our Dao[Way]," an unprecedented utterance in the history of world religion. At this point the dogmas of the established religions that one must sever one's ties with the secular world to enter priesthood are not marry collapse. Spirituality is not up there somewhere far away; it is in ordinary everyday life, in the harmonious life between husband and wife, in calm weather and prosperity of all things that result from the harmony between yin and yang forces.

---

[33] Cultivation of Women, Sermons by Divine Teacher Haewol in Dongkyungdaejeon [Eastern Great Scripture]

Conclusion

In the philosophy of Donghak, nature is believed to be a cosmic world filled with the Ultimate Energy and Spiritual Energy and it is thus believed that it should be revered as humanity and all other living things are elevated through the interconnectedness of the energy of heaven and earth.

Unlike conventional qi philosophical world views, which understand nature as a structure of energy, Donghak presents a new dimension of life in which humans experience nature as their own body and feel its pains through the cultivation of the mind. It is important to feel in our body that "all things are a manifestation of Hanullim [God] and to love by this.

As the human mind/soul is connected to all things and simultaneously bears Hanullim [God] within, life can only exist in relation to spirituality. An individual's spirituality is a tranquil empty center which cannot be touched, seen or heard, but it is in ceaseless action at the center of every creature in the universe. When engaging in brisk activities through either the body or mind, spirituality reveals itself as harmony. Spirituality's actions are realized as harmony among humans, between humanity and nature, and between human kind and Hanullim [God]. In Donghak, harmony also means harmony between femininity and masculinity and this is expressed as the harmony that lies between a wife and her husband.

Donghak does not stop at ecological awareness, but demonstrates the principals of ecological life it self. It does not look for the ultimate foundation of life in a transcendental being, but in the order and interconnected activity between heaven and earth, and the discovery of it in the spirituality within human kind which enables human to participate in life. In the Western world, God is considered to possess absolute supernatural power and is associated with masculine values. Thus God is a fearsome being and demands the submission of humans. The Western rational view granted absolute power to the constitutive power and inclinations of the human mind and developed it as a masculine proactiveness, and produced a system of socio-engineering and imperialist ideologies of domination and conquest. But in Donghak, Hanullim [God] is always compared to a parent and is addressed as the harmony between feminity and masculinity. Spirituality lies at the basis of human reason and here spirituality can be conceived as a feminine principle, like tolerance, sensitivity and tranquility. Compared with Donghak which emphasizes life and spirituality, Western civilization was founded on male-domination, rationality, and a transcendental God, rendering society one-dimensional and flat. Without a drastic change of in the character and mind/soul of human kind through a complete shift in thinking, the train headed toward the demise of humanity and the end of life cannot be stopped. Donghak provides a prototype of life requiring the comprehensive change in the framework of human consciousness and ways of living founded on a paradigm of respect in which nature is treated as one would treat either one's own body or parents.

REFERENCES

Capra, Fritjof, et al 1999, Sin-gwahak-gwa yeongseong-ui-sidae [belonging to the universe; Explorations on the Frontiers of Science and Spirituality translated by Kim Jae-hui. Seoul: Pum Yang Co.,Ltd.

Choe, Je-u. 1880. Donggyeong daejeon [Eastern Great Scripture] 1881. Yongdam Yusa [Memorial Songs of Yongdam]

Donghak Institute, Busan Arts College, ed.1999. Haewol Choe sihyeong gwa donghak sasang [Haewol, Si hyeong Choe and Donghak thought]. Seoul: Yemoonseoweon

Ham, Seokheon, tran. 1996 The bhagavad Gita. Seoul: Hangilsa, Publishing co.

Kim, Choonsung (Kim, Choonseong).2000 Donghak ui jayeon gwa saengtaejeok sam [Nature in Donghak and Ecological Life]. Donghak Hakbo[Donghak Jounal] 2001. "Yongdam yusa ui cheolhagjeog gochal" [Philosophical Reflections in Memorial songs of Yongdam]. Donghak hakbo [Donghak journal] 2.

Kim, jaehui, ed. 2000. Kkaeyeonnan yeosin[Goddess awakening] Seoul: Jeongsinsaegaesa

O, Munhwan, 1996. Sarami hanulida[Human is heaven]. Seoul: Sol Publishing Co.

Shiva, Vandana. 1998. Saranamgi[Staying alive], translated by Kang, suyeong. Seoul: Sol Publishing Co.

Whitehead, Alfred.1997. Gwanyeomui moheom [Adventure of Ideas] translated by O, Yeonghwan. Seoul: Hangilsa Publishing Co.

Yang, Zuan. 1999. Jungyongcheolhak[Philosophy of the doctrine of Mean], translated by Hwang, Gapyeon, Seoul: Seokwangsa Publishing Co.

Yi, Donhwa, ed.1993. Cheondogyo Changeonsa[The founding history of Cheondogyo], Seoul: Office of Religious Affairs, Cheondogyo Central Church

4

History of Donghak religion

4-1. The Great Master Suwoon,

-founder of Donghak

drawing portrait of
the Great Master
Suwoon

The Great Master Suwoon, the founder of Donghak[Eastern Learning, Eatern Doctrine] was born on October, 28th in 1824, at the small village of Gajeonglee, Hyungok township, in Gyeongjoo city, located in the south east area of Korea peninsula, which had been capital of old country Shilla for about decade century.

His father Choe, Ok, a poor classical scholar having literary fame among the Confucianists lived Kyungsang province. The surname of his mother was Han, a re-married household[his grand father made his father remarry for his grand father's need hoping grand son according to the social tradition of Confucianism of that era]. Great Master Suwoon, the only son of re-married mother, who was very clever enough to learn all the doctrines of Confucianism though young age, held a painful experience in his child hood because the corrupt governance of feudal society didn't permit the man born by re-married woman. Though young age, he had to live with the thought delivering people who must live with poverty, hopelessness under the utmost chaotic environment of such society, at last he made his mind to wander all country arroun to search for the wise man who could teach him the way how to relieve the poor people for a decade in his thirty ages. In Donghak Theology, they said this period of searching for the way of delivering painful people is 'the Great Master's wandering of the eight provinces'[at that times, there is eight provinces in Korea]. During his wandering he had encountered several men of ideas and religions but he couldn't find any answer to rescue the poor, painful people. After this wandering, he was getting more despondence about the world going around, on one day on spring, he had a mystical experience to be visited by a stranger with a mysterious book. [Chonseo: Book from heaven, Donghak followers called, but the contents of the book and the book itself is unavailable today]. After this meeting with a stranger, being given an odd book, his a spiritual raging thirst, and some feeling arised after reading the stranger book, made him to be prayer to heaven instead of searching some answers from others. Following this events, the great master made his mind to pray for 49 days in a small mountain hermitage called Naewonam located Yangsan area, and his pray continued according to his decision of praying. But, at near the 49th day of praying, suddenly he could recognize his father's younger brother's death during his praying continued without any artificial information, so it made him hard to pray continuously. Coming home suddenly, after stoping praying, he had got to know his uncle's sudden death on coming back home in fact. On failing his first pray for answer of salvation of the world by uncle's funeral, he made his mind restart to pray again, and he became finished to pray for 49 days at the same place. After this sincere praying finally, he had a chance to commune with Hanullim[god], the greatest important significant accident for humankind and all things in the world, at Yongdam pavilion [he had to live here for poverty, which his father had built] near the his birth place Hyungok township, on April 5th, in 1960.

After getting this amaging religious moment to commune with Hanullim, he said that it was given that the Great Way of Heaven[truth: Nothing of no return], the youngboo[figure of sprit] and the Jumoon[Invocation] by God. [ref.: nonhakmoon]. After receiving them, the great master Suwoon had had very important times near the twelve months in preparation of scriptures and training his mind, of course, he might have some chances to commune with God.

Then, on the sixth month of second year of 1861, he emerged for the first time to face the world and to spread new doctrine of virtue and goodness to the people. His doctrine is that all the people of this world is equal with the reason why they all have spirit same as Hanullim[God], so they must be served like God. And that was received with great hope by the most people who fully wanted new social patterns for improvement of their life under the worst environment to be treated inhumanely. Accordingly the area of Yongdam pavilion, where the great master lived at, got be full of people gathered from around province to hear and study the new doctrine after beginning of his speech, and all they hoped to be followers of the great master. This chance that many a people had gathered to hear new idea of new worth of life was affected those, and give them scare the established of the Confucians and the rulers. Alas! what a stupid human being's history it was, it happened the same as the tragic accident of Jesus Christ's! Because this new word had made him to be martyred in a few years. Thus, he became entrapped by the many a Confucian in the Gyungsang province and officials of ruler who had ambitions to preserver their benefits and right, therefore, in the eleventh month of the second year of Podeok[to spread God's virtue] in 1862, he finally had to depart from Yongdam as a refugee, he secluded himself in a mountain hermitage, Eunjeogam in Jeolla province located south west of Korea far from his home like a poor homeless. But in that small hermitage, in winter, he wrote the most important sacred taxt of Nonhagmoon[A discussion of learning: to be base of the Donghak theology of Hanullim], Gweonhakga[rhythmic poet to encourage for leaning neo-truth, Donghak doctrine] and Dosoosa[rhythmic poet on controlling mind].

After winter, he came back home, Yongdam, yet on going of officials suspect to arrest, at last on Desember, 10th in 1863, he got to be arrested by Jeong, Ungoo and his man, special emissary sent by the central ruler of dynasty in Hanyang[old name of Seoul]. They transported him as a prisoner to Hanyang, but at that times just to reach, suddenly poor King Chuljong[before being King, he had boyhood to gather firewood at Kanghwa island] was dead and they had to take him back to the jail of Kyungsang province. On their way back, many a followers of the great master desired to take their master back to be free, but the great master dissuaded them from doing it.

Without a plea of a suspicion, the great master obediently submitted to be tied and bound. After serving time in Daegu jail, on March, 10th in 1864, he was formally given the death sentence for an inflammatory pronouncement, and at last he was punished by beheading by the legal authorities in Gyeongsang province.

4-2. Second Master Haewol

- first successor to the leader of Donghak

He was born at the small hamlet of Hwangohri to the east of Gyungjoo, between father Choe Jongsoo a poor farmer and mother Mrs. Bae a clan of weolsung on March, 21th in 1827. His parents died at his childhood, as a orphan, on growing he had to have a lot of painful experience of non-education and poverty. After losing parents at his early age, he had to preserve his own life as a indentured farm hand, paper mill employee, slash-and -burn farmer, and so on. On a living in worst condition as the lowest class man in those society, he did never give up hope to be better some day. Fortunately he got to hear the news of hopeful doctrine from others. They said that every one who wanted to learn though poor or non-educated, welcomed and given a chance to learn somehow to rescue this chaotic world by a super master Suwoon at Yongdam area. At last he became a follower of the great master, after being a disciple, he worked in the day, while in the night he assumed with great eagerness the study and training in the master's teachings. This his ceaseless effort to study the eastern theology made him a some one who became to listen to the voice of Hanullim[God]. On August, 14th in 1863, the great master seeing his attentiveness and devotion, finally initiated him into the utmost great way of heaven[the doctrines of the eastern theology], this process of give-and-take means was accepted with the evidence of becoming successor in the Donghak religion to all of the other followers. In this way Master Haewol succeeded the Great Master Suwoon to become the second founding leader of Donghak[the Eastern Theology]. According to his teather's last order "Go far away from me!" in the jail of Daegu, he fled away into the several hermits of the high mountains located in Gangwon, Gyungsang and Choongchung provinces. During his life as a refugee, for thirty-six years of hiding, not to be captured by rulers, he did never forget all the things taught by his great teacher, and never spend his time though for one hour. He did not bide his time in hiding, but reassembled scattered followers of his great master, taught and led them instead of the late Great Master Suwoon. Even though he was lurking about the country, he had exerted himself to the utmost to practice as his teacher did, and so day by day, the number of followers got to increase more and more. Naturally, he felt the necessities of many a text of his master's doctrine, he collected and compiled the assorted religious writings of late teacher, and had them published in two separate volumes which was entitled Donggyungdaejeon[Scriptures of Donghak] and Yongdamyoosa[Rhythmic poets of Yongdam] with wooden printing block, thus the greatest doctrine for human written by the great master Suwoon who had a heart-to-heart communication with Hanullim[God]. At last by his holy effort, Donghak halls(home could be used as church, occasionally) had spread throughout the country. In order to consolidate to learn his teacher's doctrine more, Master Haewol restored the country wide system for efficient management of organization of scatterd Donghakian halls[some different from church: in the point of view of the eastern theology].

In order that he had exonerted his great master from the guilty to be entrapped by Confucian, he mobilized thousands of Donghakist[Donghak followers] in a protest against the rulers of dynasty, but it didn't be permited that their reasonable demand to the Gojong, king of last but one of Lee's dynasty, who gave up his right and responsibility to protect his people and nation by the unreasonable requisition of Japanese, in spite of preserving long history of keeping nation from the invations of the strong China and the Mongol empire.

At that era, some western countries requested to open the door diplomatically, and to correspond with them by armed ship to the closed dynasty. Then, Japanese which had been receiving benefits of culture of Korean for long times before the Restoration of Meiji was modernized earlier than Korea and China by acceptance of new technique to make weapon and ship from western country. Thus modernized Japanese having ambition to invade the continent, colonized benevolent neighbor to extort diplomatic right from King Gojong with lies and deception coated with friendship. [After several years, Japan started an aggressive war to China and Russia, at last such a endless greedy leaders of such a Jap. attacked the Pearl harbour bestially without a declaration of war. How dirty tricks they were!] In that era, many unarmed Donghak believers to resist against tyranny of officials of Chosun dynasty, and most of them were killed by Japanese soldier's machine gun, and continuously many family of them were killed by officials of Chosun dynasty and Jap. Soldiers, to whom King Gojong requested to kill his unarmed people with the only reason for having new idea and religion. In the Korean history that accident was written Donghak movement, and the accident became the origin of the China-Japanese war. After Donghak movement, Master Haewol, the great second leader of Donghak followers was captured, and starved near to death for his faith, with saying that he could not have a honourable death of beheading as his teacher, but finally they rejected his last hope, and he was beheaded to death as the Great Master Suwoon, in 1898. Here I felt with the greatest humility from Master Haewol same as Saint Peter's the greatest humility to his teacher Jesus Christ. And Honourable Master Haewol who had a spirit chastened by suffering had revived Donghak religious group among the crisis of dynasty's depression and guided them to be established to great religion for new era.

4-3. Donghak movement

In Korea history, the Donghak movement have had the great significance as a bridge to connect the idea of democracy grown among the peoples naturally through the long era of the dynasty of King to the modern democratic nation named Korea. The most peoples in the world, in a certain point of view, might think that the eastern democracy might be influenced from the western citizenship came over to the east asia, but in case of Korea, though the republic nation could be built with the help of UN after World War II, the history of Korean democracy being different from other Asian countries, originated to the Donghak movement. If the King and the established of Chosun dynasty had changed their mind to the Dognhak's idea without depression their movement, I am sure that there had had been no sorrowful history to give up the diplomatic right to Jap. Yes, the Donghak movement was a people's resistant movement to the dynasty for human's right for living, freedom, and equality just like the Grand Revolution of France though it failed. If we can find the origin of the grand revolution of France from the idea of Christianism, Donghak movement have to be undertood another grand revolution with the origin of Donghakism(or Shicheonjuism)[34] of Suwoon's doctrine in Korea about 100 years ago, which is the idea that all the lives have spirituality ought to be esteemed. Thus voluntary movement of peoples for human's right being

---

[34]   Shicheonjuism(Donghakism): The best important idea of Donghak that all things have spirit, and the highest spirit among them is humanbeings', which was said by Suwoon.

resistant to the King's absolute right with numerous victims only could be found in upper two countries in the recent history of politics. But we have to know the differentiation between upper two accident, in the point of view that one had the political purpose to built new country, but the other had religionary purpose only for the society in which peoples could live with reverence each other, so if say strictly, Donghak movement is not revolution for political purpose, but only movement for human right living as they were taught by Suwoon. And it is in the right to call the victims of Donhak movement not to be revolutioners but to be martyrdoms.

4-4. After Master Haewol's martyrdom

The most Korean modern native religions were formed with the basic idea of upper two men's doctrine, especially Cheondogyo and Suwoongyo are main stream of Donghakgian, but in a certain point of view, they all have some differences to the original idea of great two Master's doctrine. Both were showed some Buddhismic character after Haewol's martyrdom. For example, they are all hope to reach to some mental state toward eternal life at peace, so they insist that 'relief your spirit without body' and they have made abnormal religious trend to afflict their body for misleading of their new masters, In fact, such a religious misleading have been showed in Catholic history and Buddhism history for long era over twenty century.

This religious phenomenon of misleading human kind is thought to have originated to few leaders of religion, misunderstanding absolute being or in governors wanting political profit for him. If we think this idea with common sense, in our history, nobody could show us the world of eternal life and eternal peace. They have said that we could enter that ideal world after death, but if we think again with deep insight they all have made wrong image to be true for their individual purpose.

We have to remember what Jesus said, "Act good and you shall go to heaven, if not, you shall go to hell.", in this sentence we have to recognize that the upper sentence have the truth of "the result become followed according to what we have had done." What do we identify this sentence truly means? Is this word means truely the ideal world after death? One of genius philosopher, Niche had insisted that most of philosophers and theologists in his era were out of mind, after getting special experience. On the contrary, did he be a crazy man as they said?

Ultimatey, the Donghak theology that is new term in the world, it can be given that the sufficient value to be explorated as religious theory of Suwoon and Haewol's doctrine with the view of science and philosophy, and to make it sure that what the reality of God is and how we can commune with the reality, what the effect will appear after communion with reality. Now humankind have get new era to live with the real diety not with abstract God.

5

To commune with Holy Spirit[God]

5-1. Training mind

Our great master Suwoon said that God have no shape but only make some trajectory, with the truth of nothing of no return, and the truth[Hanulim, God] do not have the specificity of movement, stationariness and changing of itself, but have the nature of fullness, emptiness, alternation and succession. [*ref: nonhagmoon] In this point of view, I think that the process of controlling mind[training mind] might be a just the process of gathering the scattered mam-factors through all the cells and organs of our body to heart connected to the involuntary nervous system of brain.

In order to understand the training mind, which is special significance in Donghak [the eastern religion] according to the doctrine of the eastern theology, is very important. After the historical communiction with Hanullim(Korean language of God like in the Bible) at the time of the April 5th, 1960, Suwoon the Great Master said to all of the followers to keep the mind as pure and immaculate as born without any greed at first. And he said that the all of the human beings need to train mind. This doctrine means the all of the human being is contaminated with immoral desires. Here we have to give attention to this doctrine that was given by God, as the scripture of the master's descriptions. And than, the most important massage from God for all human beings, is the way how to train their mind. That is to repeat the Jumoon [invocation] given by Hanullim with integrity, respect and faith and than you will receive the holy spirit, and energy of

69

Hanullim[God]. The Jumoon[invocation] composed of only 21's letters of the meaning word.[35]

The Great Master, Suwoon said that you do not need to pray and to look for me but for Hanullim, directly. [We can find this sentence at the yongdamyoosa, the poem with rhythm that written in Korean letters by himself.] We have to recognize and apprehend that the relationship can be formed between God and human being not via church or minister but via individual mind. (This doctrine to be given by Hanullim[God] showed the crucial different point between the western theology[Christianism] and the eastern theology[Donghakism].) Accordingly the salvation of the humankind will be completed not massively but individually as the Master said. The course of the training mind, to repeat the two invocations 21 letters of Ji Gi Gum Ji Won Wee Dae Gang(8 terms of the invocation for coming down of holy spirit and energy.), and Si Cheon Ju Jo Wha Jung Yeong Sae Bool Mang Man Sa Ji (13 terms of the main invocation), loudly or silently only with the mind of integrity, respect and faith. Many of Donghakian(The Great Master's followers, who believed in Hanullim[God] showed by the Great Master, Suwoon, in Korea) had experience to commune with holy spirit, during this training course. About this phenomenon, many philosophers and psychologists have predicated super natural or mystical experience. You can read this in detail at the chapter of the experience of holy spirit.

5-2. For what we have to control mind

The way how to control mind had been taught by the Great Master Suwoon, and which was requested by God according to the his memorial. It is God's order for mankind to control mind, and than one will get long life.

---

[35]   About this letter, usually they said Chinese, but in the ancient period Korean ancestors had made it and gave up to use by passing era because it was not proper Korean's language and pronunciation system, in this point of view there had been the evidence of the our ancestor's doctrine of concept of Hanullim[God] on the turtle's crust to be written about 6-7000 years ago to be estimated with meaning word same as the old chinese letter, for example, Cheonbugyung written with these phasic letterforms.

It is very important that God's word of "getting long life" not going to Heaven, which was said to Suwoon, because the existence called God is just a real being in this world not abstract being above the sky or heaven.

Here we could find out that to control mind is to be a chance to purify our greedy mind which had been contaminated during our living in this society after getting the ability of recognition. It's very similar to Zen meditation, without reciting jumoon[invocation] of 21 letters. But the most important different distinction comparing the both, the former was taught by God, the latter was made by man. Many believers of Donghak [let's call them Donghakians] who had got a mystic experience to get health and wisdom, similar to be ecstasy, said that it is hard to express with a word, and recommend training mind as Suwoon's doctrine, and you can feel some difference.

But they all would say that they felt some change of the body and mind after getting special experience to commune with holy sprit through training mind. For example, If I write the change physiologically, some one felt getting health, others who was discomfortable became good condition, a bald man got hair grown, a sterile woman became pregnant. They all have believed that their experience was a amaging phenomenon of holy spirit of God. And to conclude, through the process of the controlling mind, our spirit could become one together to Hanullim's holy spirit though it's an amazing experience in an instant. Most of all, a amazing change of our mind to the pure spirit have had appeared continuously after getting the special experience to commune with Holy Spirit, he might be a lier to deceive his neighbor and himself.

5-3. To receive Youngboo

-to draw spirit as a symbolic figure

Some of Donghakians who had a special experience communing with holy spirit, would have a more special experience getting a chance to draw Youngboo [figure of spirit] during controlling mind, it happened as below. Suddenly one had a overwhelming desire to draw something during controlling mind, and he got to call some instrument of drawing and paper, and than he drew some shape on the paper after getting drawing instruments. Here we can see the Youngboo sample drawn by Mrs. Junghee Han, who lives in Anyang city,

Gyunggi province which was got during her controlling mind at the training center. Fortunately, I got a chance to see that Mrs. Han drew the Youngboo, and I could take photos what she drew at the controlling mind center. For readers' understanding of these youngboo, my thought about her youngboo attached below.

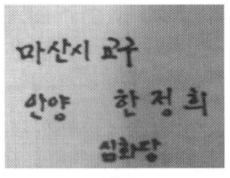

F

F: Drawer's name of Mrs. Junghee Han and her address written in Korean by herself

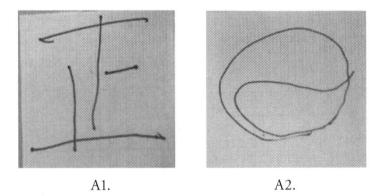

A1.   A2.

A1: Old letter using in Korea and China originated from pictograph, which means the right morallity and honesty.

A2: Taegeug shape figure, the same shape is showed at the center of Korean flag which is the image of the origin of cosmic alternation containing yin-and-yang factors in Suwoon's doctrine.

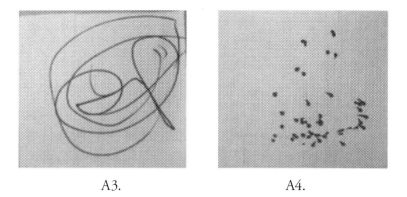

A3.   A4.

A3: This figure seems to be a certain stage of alternation of cosmos.

A4: This figure seems to be many galaxies or small universes being scattered as parts of universe.

6

Suwoon's doctrine

- The Greatest Creator of Donghak religion

6-1. To understand Hanullim[God] by Suwoon

The great master, Suwoon said the character of Hanullim at the description he wrote. In the scriptures of Donggyungdaejeon, [Mr. Haewol second master, the great master's best follower collected, had had preserved the papers that his teacher wrote after the greatest master's martyrdom, and published them under the ground at the era of persecution of the bureaucracy in the last dynasty, on 19 century in Korea, with the name of the book Donggyungdaejeon.] We can read what the character of God is at the chapter of the Podugmoon part. I hope that the man who have interest in the new massage of God have to read Suwoon's doctrines attached.

At the Nonhagmoon chapter in Donggyungdaejeon, there we can look for the three characters of God; the great master said that the all of them were given by God [Hanullim]. The first character is holy spirit, which is the same quality with spirit(heart, pure mind) of all lives created in this world as human being's, the second is the extreme energy[the cause of existence of universe, the origin of vital power], the third is the truth of nothing of no return. About the holy spirit, at the Nonhagmoon chapter, Hanullim said to the great master Suwoon, at that time to commune with at first "your mind is my mind".

Today, the many scholars of philosophy and psychology, and brain science agree with that the mind is same meaning as the mental function, same as herat and spirit, and so the above sentence can be changed to "your spirit is my spirit". And the great master said the human being is one who have the most superlative spirit of all of the creatures. This comparative expression could imply that the all of the lives should have spirit though they are lower level than human beings'. Such a amazing doctrine which we men have never heard, is the Donghak theology which might be a view of new world that the all creatures have the vital value, spirit which originated to God and given by God same as mankind.

The second character is the extreme energy[the greatest power]. It is the cause of the universe formation and the existence of all, and the origin of movement and alternation. But we mankind can't understand them and simply count the great Energy of Spirit with our intuition, and so the sentence of the scripture of "God have no shape but makes some trajectory [The Hanul (God) is formless but has traces: Nonhagmoon]" can be understood as the record of the character of the greatest energy of God. Third character, the truth of "nothing of no return," same as upper two identities of God, is the greatest specificity which has never been known to human being. This truth that could be understood as the causation doctrine of Buddhism, the cyclical theory of energy of the physics and the cyclical change of nature, is the principle of the creation, variation and alternation of persona and universe. We can see similar expression of the sentence of "I am alpha and omega." at the Bible. Many a western theologian have had thought that this Jesus' word means "I am beginner and finisher." only with the superficial and the second dimensional view point. But here let's think about such thought, all of us can know God is not the second dimensional existence, but the most of Christian predicate as such way. More over, for this point of view, it could be thought that the eschatology which most christians have had believed in, might be produced in early stage of Roman Catholic. I dare think the omega have to be thought with the state of over lapping to the alpha spatially like spiral pattern because the Cosmos must be recognized with over tridimensional structure not with two dimensional one. So I dare guess that the reason of the eschatology would be originated to such misinterpretation of Jesus' speech by miscomprehension of that word by the some priest who lived in 1,700 years ago.

The evidence of my thought can be found with the Lord's Prayer at Bible, on searching the sentence of "thy kingdom come, on earth as it is in heaven".

Such doctrine of Jesus shows us that the most important point of view about God, is not fantastic existence to meet after death but realistic one living with us, which can come down to earth and live with us as a real being in and out our body. If we think with deep insight, for understanding this clause of Lord's prayer, firstly, that clause must be recognized with our reasonable thought and we must answer to the question written below. Which is reasonable between "thy kingdom coming down on earth" and "building thy kingdom on earth with thee"? And how do we think that thy kingdom could be moved to earth? In spite that we know the most clauses in Bible written with many metaphoric expression, we have had accepted that some clauses must be true as it was written. How foolish we are!

Many sentences of the Bible described God is holy spirit, light and truth of alpha and omega, and than our great master said that Hanullim[God] have three characters of holy spirit, the greatest energy and truth of nothing of no return. Here we can find that their doctrines are very similar, and according to their doctrine it could be natural that we can understand the most of questions in the world, which our recognition could reach to. For this reason, I have had tried to understand all the question that I have biologically, psychologically, philosophically and in physics with concerned books written by the scientists and philosophers.

Finally, through the doctrine of Donghak[the eastern theology] it might be reasonable that the identities of diety can be understood as the character of God being a reality to be composed with three special characters, spirit, energy and truth. And the most important point of view is that this complexed character of God's identity is showed by Godself through the great master at the small old village near Kyungjoo area, in 1860 in Korea. But we could not find any mysterious and fantastic things in his doctrines, so all which might be a reality except Communion with God. we mankind have had used to think that God might be some existence without reality for long period over many thousand years. And than, what made us to be misunderstood with God's real characters? I dare say it might be the reason for the ignorance of undeveloped man. But now days, we human become wiser enough to develop all the fields of modern science, and metaphysics. With such developed modern science, with high cognitive ability, and with pure spirit, and with pure reason which can be recognized by modern intelligence, now in this era we man have to try again to understand what the reality of God is.

Because such exploration will give us a chance to think deeply about the questions what we human beings are, what the righteous relationship with neighbors is, and what the righteous way to live is, for peace, for hope of ourselves and for the next generation. And the truth of trinity of spirit, energy and truth of nothing of no return have been acceptable not to Old Trinitarian of Catholicism but to all human kind as the reasonable reality of New Trinitarian.

6-2. To Approach with biological science

At the Bible, Matthew and John wrote that God is spirit as Jesus said, and Suwoon said so as well, as the scriptures written by himself.

But among the western, through the many a century of middle age, the theologians of Christianity have had thought the identity of God, as the spirit to be a some existence of super being not to be belong to human, despite that some sentences that spirit is in man showed at Bible, but few imphirists of philosophers had tried to search for it in man, one of them, the genius philosopher, Descartes, Kant had thought that the spirit is the mind and heart in man though he expressed it as "reason" or "pure reason". Nowadays we usually accept that there are not any different meanings between the spirit and the mind over the west and the east.

With that thought, many psychologists had tried to identify the mind in man, according to the development of psychology, at last the brain science got appeared as a new field of the psychology, and the brain scientists have tried to find out reality of God with brain, but they have showed us only action potentials of brain tissue and neurons. Here, we have to think about growing process of the infant in the uterus of mother's. Because to observe the process of life growing of fetus period could become to understand forming mind and beginning mind function at the primitive stage of life. In all the text of the physiology, we can find that the brain's electrical wave appears after cardiac function in about three months. How can we understand this pattern of infant's growing? Don't this show the steps of growing of infant's organ to be our mistake to understand the origin of life? More over the heart can have function without brain, but brain don't have any function without heart's pumping in vitro examinations. Generally we believe that God would be the origin of life, as some factor of forming life with truth, if not we human kind might have had betrayed by them who told us God to be life. In biology all the lives are composed of cells of the smallest biological unit, and in physics all the materials are made of molecules of the smallest particle of physical unit. And cell is composed of numerous molecules formed with atoms. And all atoms is composed of proton, neutron, and electron. In physiology, the life phenomenon of vital energy alteration is belonging to electrons. This electronic magnetic theory became some evidence of original factors of life in physics, and in physiology. As they said, if God [Hanullim: spirit] is the origin of life and of this world, it ought to be find some specificity of God in all the beings. Because the being created and the creator have to be one in the cosmos, if not, it is not reasonable to think some existence to make this great universe. If anybody think like that, he might live in the supper material world, and he must live without any food, and so it is in the wrong logically and scientifically that the existence theory of dualism they insisted. So I became to think the utmost fine factor, if there were something like that to

be thought to be origin of electron and life phenomenon it could be called mam-factor as spirit factor or mind factor as the hypothesis written above. But evidently, we can not have any analytical interpretation about that, and so we don't have any evidence of searching for and identifying it yet, but some of scientists must be able to understand that my thought seems to be reasonable.

6-3. To Approach with Kant's philosophy

One of the eastern idea, there was a book of Daodejing, which was known to be written by Lau-tzi or others, [certainly it was made and appeared after his death by his followers, and have came down through the long era. ref: Daodaejing] The book showed the image of the Cheon might be a great power with mind [very similar to Donghak's doctrine except truth].

In Europe, several famous philosophers had tried to certify the reality logically. Among them, we have to notify two philosophers of German, Nietche and I. Kant, because they had tried to show us some identity for the origin of virtue against to the authoritarian Catholicism of the social and religious ideology of their era. Genius philosopher Nietzsche had denied all the idea of former philosophers and he had insisted that we could understand reality not with theological knowledge and philosophical logics but only with emotion and intuition. And another greatest philosopher in history, I. Kant, a philosopher insisting that we had to find our pure reason instead of God of Christianity. His wisdom being over and above the period could meet new theology of Donghak, which claimed that all lives have spirit in. Some body might think the differentiation of 'pure reason' and 'spirit'. If we don't have an insight of our mental function of brain, 'pure reason' of Kant's word can't be understood physiologically in brain science. Usually we must think that it can be acceptable image only with metaphysical logics, and so the image of 'pure reason' can be known as a pure state of our mind without any greed. In fact, this state of our mind can be thought only in babyhood and infanthood physiogically. In this stage, the act of baby and infant must be only the instinctive behavior which do not originate to the coginitive development of brain. If we think the origin of infant's life to be spirit, the Kant's word of 'pure reason' become very similar meaning with spirit as the early stage of individual life's growing. Here I dare say that the word of 'pure reason' of I. Kant can be thought to be the another name of 'spirit,' in the point of view that the both are the origins of life, To understand the meanings written above, let's think about infant's action, it is thought to be only the instinctive action without the recognition of brain, in other word, it is the stage not to appear the recognition function of brain, of course, we can't find any action of greed in fetus hood and in infanthood. So we can call "the reason" of this stage's brain function to be "pure reason" physiologically and philosophically as Kant's image.

More over his virtue of 'categorical imperative' showed at 'the critique of practical reason' is just same as Suwoon's doctrine of 'myung-do' which means 'order of our spirit doing righteous as the bright virtue of natural way' and as God's order in Jesus' doctrine. We have to take notice to I. Kant because his logical arguments have a great value of virtue of spirituality. By insight, we can agree the 'a priori', one of Kant's key word is origin of 'pure reason', so if not the image of 'a priori', no image of 'pure reason' can be told. As we know these two terms are abstractive noun, so they are can not identified with physiologically in our brain, But if we think with more deep insight with modern science, 'a priori' can be suggested with DNA, and 'pure reason' can be suggested with very early infanthood state of brain's recognition function as well, because in adulthood it is impossible to definite brain function of 'pure reason' except several men like Buddha, Jesus, Nietche, Kant and Suwoon and few men who had had pure spirit not to be contaminated with greed for their lives in our history. These propositions of him were derived from natural law as he said. The terms of 'categorical imperative' and 'free volition' are very similar image of 'order of God' and 'free will of no greedy heart showing in babyhood which clause we can find in Bible, and in Suwoon's and Buddha's doctrine', and in a certain state of Tao. His greatest theoretical idea of the logical truth all he said, could be found in human being, not in God of the Bible. As the descriptions written above, he was the first man who explored spirituality in human, in ourselves though he explained it with the terms of 'a priori' and 'pure reason', and certainly he opened new horizon to the mankind with searching for true virtue and true beauty standing at human side not God's side.

These his great idea was brightened by another great man, Suwoon born in the eastern small country Korea, with the doctrine given by Hanullim [Korean name of God] after his death about 100 years, in which he said that to all human and the lives, spirit was given with the same as God's spirit at birth naturally by Hanullim[God].

But now days, in America, a new idea to understand reality was argued by Husserl and White Head in the field of philosophy. The superiority of their philosophy could be accepted, in order to find out the reality from not only our recognition but physical world. Because the word of 'the reality' have meaning of existence of itself in the world, and in future, I believe that we can recognize it with the three proofs of ontological, cosmological, and physico-theological which said by Kant, [36] some day by the some utmost genius and wise philosophical physicist.

> In a famous section, Kant set to work to demolish all the purely intellectual proofs of existence of God. He makes it clear that he has other reasons for believing in God; these he was to set forth later in 'The critique of Practical reason'. But for the time being his purpose is purely negative. There are, he says, only three proofs of God's existence by pure reason; these are the ontological proof, the cosmological proof, and the physico-theological proof.

---

[36]   Modern philosophy: 709p.

The ontological proof, as he set it forth, defines God as the 'ens realissimum' the most real being; i.e. the subject of all predicates that belong to being the "existence" is such a predicate, this subject must have the predicate "existence," i.e., must exist. Kant objects that existence is not a predicate. A hundred thalers that I merely imagine may, he says, have all the same predicate as a hundred real thalers.

The cosmological proof says; if anything exists, then an absolutely necessary

Being must exists, now I know that I exist; therefore an absolutely necessary Being exists, and this must be the 'ens realissimum'. Kant maintains that the last step in this argument is the ontological argument over again, and that is therefore refuted by what has been already said. [In upper sentence, it might be better for us to accept Kant's opinion to be that "I know that cosmos is exist; therefore absolute necessary Being must exists, and this must be the "ens realissimum." / writter's thought]

The physico-theological proof is the familiar argument from design, but in metaphysical dress. It maintains that the universe exhibits an order which is evidence of purpose. This argument is treated Kant with respect, but he points out that, at best, it proves only Architect, not a Creator, and therefore cannot give an adequate conception of God. He concludes that "the only theology of reason which is possible is that which is based upon moral laws or seeks guidance from them."

[In upper sentence, 'physico-theological proof' might mean the physical proof of God in theology, because we are sure the fact that Kant knew theology must be a metaphysical theory already, so he might want to say "the physical mechanism of creation in theology, not architect." / writter's thought]

6-4. To approach with physical hypothesis

Many admired physicists were born and contributed the development of human's life historically. We must have great regards for them as much as we can do for the greatest men of Jesus, Kant and Suwoon. Because we know that the development of culture and civilization can have had been going forward by all of them. The Newton's laws of motion and Einstein's principle of relativity would be a part of the great rule of God's truth of "nothing of no return" which Suwoon's doctrine showed.

And Faraday, Maxwell gave us the special knowledge of the universal specificity of the greatest alternation of Hanullim[god] of Suwoon's doctrine with the theory of electro-magnetic field. But so far they didn't find out the reality of God just as Jesus and Suwoon did not know physics. In the Cosmology, the black hole theory and big bang theory become reliable recognition to the most people, though they are not certified yet. And in microphysics, very small particle called Higg's particle become the object of our interest, but yet it can not be found out certainlly, in spite of that several times of experiment have done by some of excellent physicist's approach under the mathematical hypothesis. We can meet a questionable constant in the text of physics, some physicists could count the mysterious constant number of 10^{-40} with mathematical method, and they threw it to physicists who have been exploring universal and micro physics. But nobody can answer to this question of identity of 10^{-40} constant so far.

If there were some very small substances like factor written above in size, or in weight, it must never be evident by human being in near future, because we can know the experimental limitation of micro-physics. This book can be written with the hypothesis that the very super micro size of 10^{-40} might exist, and let's call it mam-factor, which might shaped right triangular corn form or pyramid form which have translucent, flexible membrane-like-wall because they might have special specificity to change easily to adhere line to line, plate to plate to make space and time with increasing total volume and numbers by self division like virus which have common character with duality of life-matter.

6-5. To approach with the Donghak theology

6-5-1. The Cosmology

In Donggyoungdaejeon which was written by the greatest master Suwoon, we could find some significant word about cosmology. If we would accept the the words directly without any analogical interpretation of the metaphor, we could understand nothing with his doctrine, because all the scriptures of religion written with many a metaphoric expression. And I prayed to Hanullim and controlled my mind every times when I met the questions being hard to recognize what written at the scriptures in order to get some wisdom to understand what they mean. I think it would be some dangerous, and hazardous for me to talk about the Cosmology with the eastern theology because I am not cosmologist and physicist. But I determined to talk about the Cosmos as I recognized with freedom and courage given by Hanullim after praying not to make me misunderstand Hanullim[God] but to make me recognize the identity and reality.

We can find the word goong-goong [podeokmoon] like puzzle as the drawing holy spirit which certified by Hanullim[God] through the greatest master Suwoon. The sentence of expressing goong-goong in the scripture is showed, as below. [ref: podeokmoon: I asked him, Hanullim, "Do you mean that I shall teach people with the western doctrine[Christian: Catholic] of God?" and than she said, "No, I have a young-boo [figure of holy spirit] which is called Seonyak[Hanull's medicine]. Its shape is tae-geug[the symbol of the great ultimate alternation of universe: and the yin-yang is the image of factors of alternation] and its form is also like goong-goong, as well. [goong means bow and so goong-goong is the shape of two bows]. Please receive my young-boo of spirit and cure humankind's disease with it. And also receive my Jumoon[invocation] and teach people with it for me. And let the virtue of mine spread to all human beings over the world, and you shall have long life." In astrophysics, we can see the picture of the great universe to be drawn to the shape of a rugby ball by astrophysicist using electronic and optical science. And we can find a central white string like pattern from one side of pole to another. [ref: Galaxies in the universe. writers: L.S.Sparke & J.S.Gallagher]

Here if we make some shape in the space with the two bows(arcs), putting string to string each other, and than the end part of two arc will become two poles, and turn around them conterclockwise with the state of one pole down on to the ground, and than we can fined tridimensional shape like a rugby ball in the space.. And there showed a narrow tunnel from one pole to the other pole formed by strings of two arcs. And if the tunnel shape really formed by tornado phenomenon of the cosmic scale of mam-factor turning around by itself continuously, that could have special electromagnetic trait of physics, and that could be a origin of the movement and alternation of cosmos.

If you were God having four dimensional specificity as the origin of universe, how could you tell your shape to human beings who have three dimensional character and have to live in the limited space and time?

In the universe there could never exist like the human shaped God. [ref: man is the only existence to have the highest spirit in nature: nonhakmoon] And than, somebody would be foolish to try to search for E.T. in mistaking it for God, if there were E.T. he might say to man "Sorry but I am not God." And so I think the metaphoric word goong-goong means the shape of the greatest universe. And next, what taegeug means? The word of the taegeug is defferent with the yinyang, the yinyang is the word meaning mechanism of alteration, but the taegeug means the shape of movement to be produced by the greatest energy of cosmos, as a being origin of alternation.[37] There is no direction of formal range for recognition of the yinyang, but the taegeug have a image having direction of rotation movement counterclockwise. [If you want, You can see the taegeug shape at the center circle colored with red and blue at the national flag of Korea.]

And the second question is what this form of universe should be made. I wrote my thought from now. On writing this chapter, the first of all I dare pray that if I would mistake, please Hanullim [God] forgive me. I will write with different letters when I write what I recognized during praying, controlling mind, because I have no evidence of physics to show to my readers. To the respected readers of this book, if you would meet any sentence not to be understood please send me via internet mail to choe0828@naver..com and you will receive some answer of my thought from me though I am not a physicist,

---

[37]   If we think that the Taegeug is the symbol of the original array of the energy, drown with two color of yin and yang, which will be the origin of alteration. There might be some differentiation between two space of yin and yang. If we think this shape with the array of energy, the upper position must be get a bigger positional energy, comparing with below positional energy. And if we think about electro-magnetice energy, the upper space might have smaller energy than below space. These differentiation of energy will be the origin of the alterative movement in cosmos. / writer

6-5-2. About Creator

- Reality of Hanullim[God],

- Truth originate to Taekeuk-yin and yang

In fact, it is very hard to write about the reality of God, because many theologians, philosophers and scientists have tried to find the reality, but none of them can definite it exactly so far, so I dare approach with logical exploration of comparing two scriptures which was written with special experience of two Holy men, Jesus and Suwoon, to commune with God in our religious history.

In Bible [written by the followers of Jesus, in 3-400yrs after his death], we can read the sentences that God created man and all in the universe just as God have human character. In Donggyungdaejon[written by Suwoon by himself], we can find the sentences in which the Creator is not a being having human character exept spirit, but a being having the ability to create all beings and universe. [ref: Bulyeongiyeon chapter]

Here we can see the deferent point of view whether creator would be thought to be some being having human character or not. But, in spite of this differentiation, their ability of creation, their power to alternate universe and their identity of spirit are same, and their truth to be said is very similar. [One said it alpha and omega, another said it nothing of no return, these two image become same. Because we can recognize that God is not plane dimensional being, but over three dimensional being.] And than, what is the reason of these differentiations that they showed? The answer to this question might be thought the reason of different ability of people's intelligence to understand truth of each era with the gap about 2,000 years. If some body told the oldest knowledge of 2,000 years ago, to the mankind of modern era who have the higher intelligence of ultimately developed civilization enough to know the most truth of natural phenomenon with the exploration of micro and macro physics, embryology, electromagnetic and quantum physics, biology, physiology, neurology and so on, the audience might treat him to be a man who might be out of mind. Yes, that is another truth, the time make man change to adapt to changing environment. If we think with deep insight, it could be right that God make man to be changed, if not mankind shall be perished. We mankind have had the knowledge that God is special spiritual being except atheist, and than it ought to be that God might feel needs to make man to be changed to adopt to the new environment of changing Cosmos, and that is natural law which was said by C. Darwin.

If all sentences written above were true, God must send us new selected counselor who have to reinterpret his massages again with the word of modern Civilization for modern era's human being to protect the perishment of this world. Here let's talk about salvation, the thought that the word of salvation in Bible means usually the relief of spirit, but how God can relieve our spirit, for example, in Catholic, they said that it could become real with taking a piece of cookie, and with the believers confession to the father, and with a baptism ceremony just before death, certainly it might be some effect to make the minds of believers comfortable, psychologically. Thus methodology of salvation, entirely depending on the other, could be reasonable only to the men lived two thousand years ago. The concept of mercy and punishment is belong to the idea of human being, the deity never have the hands of mercy or hammer for punishment. There is only the truth of God, so called, the will of God, that is the strict truth of nothing of no return [Suwoon's doctrine], so if somebody have done good he will get good result, or anybody have done bad he will get the bad result. Accordingly, for God, as a being of spirit itself, he could commune with other spirit, only in case that both are pure enough to become one without any resistence. To become one means that to be unitizing with both spirit in the state of being same quality as spirit formed with mam-factor with my hypothesis. Training one's mind to become pure state of spirit in which one can commune with God, Suwoon called this course soo-ryun(controlling mind), and called the just unitized state kang-ryung(spirit's coming down) and to reach to this state. He taught his followers to recite the jumoon of 21 letters of Ji Gi Gum Ji Won Wee Dae Gang, Si Cheon Ju Jo Wha Jung Yeong Sae Bool Mang Man Sa Ji with voice or silence to commune with the Holy Spirit.

After exploration of all the descriptions in Donggyungdaejon which was written by Suwoon, I could recognize that the three kinds of identity of God[Hanullim] are the greatest utmost energy, the spirit[heart], and the truth of "nothing of no return." By the third identity of God, truth of nothing of no return, it could be understood that the reason why the all of alternation phenomenon have had appeared through the endless time in the world. Finally, Hanullim [God] might be full in the universe, in all the lives, all things, as finest heart factor, forming our mind, forming life phenomenon, forming all the materials, and might be the utmost greatest energy, and might be a truth of this alteration itself in the world. Accoring to the doctrine of the Donghak theology, Hanullim[God] have no character of human being except spirit[heart],

Here we have to definite what the human character is. Certainly we can't say that the spirit is only character of human being. Usually we call some being without body to be ghost. [here we could understand Hanullims' comment to Suwoon, "Ghost is me, too.": ref. nonhagmoon, and similar sentence in Bible]

If so, how can we understan the human-like God's image which the most Western have had thought? Here we must think the behaviors of human beings who lived at the old era without any knowledge of the universe and the physics.

In human being's brain, by the action potential's interface, two main functions of emotion and recognition appeared with complex state. If they had no information about something, they usually regarded all informations getting with upper two functions to be true. Naturally they had a tendency of selfish motives to judge some thing which they met at first, if not they must feel fear against it. And for the purpose of protection against the unknown opposite, it need for them to make something to help them which was stronger than their power. That was the reason why the old religions appeared as we know.

Accordingly, along with the tribe, the many old religions have had appeared in history, one of them, the clever tirbe called Jew, the weakest tribe, comparing their neighbors, made their guard man-shaped image, and it was getting spread after Jesus with the Bible in which he called God to be Father. And now the most people who believe in God of Christianism on the earth, must think God to be human-shape.

Now, modern sitizens who live among the environment of the best civilization and culture, must think of God's shape as the reasonable one.

As showed above, the image of God which formed with 'human like being' by our ancients who had the undeveloped intelligence, and it have been coming down from generation to generation. But now, in this our generation, we have to make the image of God to be right from the mistake which was made by our undeveloped ancients, with the greatest courage, and we have to brighten the truth of God for our next generations who follow us with belief, for development of new era of cosmic civilization.

And then, what do we think the creator is? I think that the creator called God might be existence having upper three characters of utmost energy of force, spirit and truth as Suwoon said. Generally we have known that the word God might be intrinsic noun like a person's name which have human character as the common knowledge of western, but I dare insist the word God is material qualities noun, just like water, because if we think that God create all beings in the universe as a person-like being, we have to answer to the next questions that what the first material is, and where God can take it from, and how God can make it. If we can change our old image of identity of human characteristic God to the new image of the greatest being composed of mam-factor filled in the great universe as a being having some quality and quantity, and all the phenomenon in the universe will be understood reasonably, as the contents of descriptions with my hypothesis written above. With all of upper sentences that I wrote, the reality of God could be identified as the utmost fine being having spirituality called mam-factor, with which filled in all things and universe, and it have had been increasing accountably in Cosmos. This natural phenomenon might be originor of the time and the space, originor of the black holes and big-bangs whch could create the great universe, the small universes and the galaxies. I dare insist with my hypothesis that that might be a originor of birth and death, and a being which could penetrate atom of materials and cell of the all lives without any resistence. And I dare give it the name of God [Hanullim] to the originor (being of origin)of all.

7

Haewol's doctrines

- Great second leader of Donghak religion

7-1. Truth and energy [force] of heaven and earth

The ancient said that the heaven and the earth is only a drop of water. Before the creation of the heaven and the earth of this world, there was water as the great yin at north pole of universe.*1)

Water is the origin of all the creatures. in water, there are two kind of water, yang water and **yin** water, only **yang** water which we human being could see, but yin water could not.

It is similar for fish to live in deep water as for man to live in yin water, and so human being can't recognize yin water as fishes can't feel yang water among yang water by themselves, you

portrait of Sir Haewol

should find the profound reason after having a chance to recognize something brightly with wisdom after communing with Holy spirit with the experience of controlling mind. One of Followers asked what the sun and the moon was created from. He answered that the sun is the essence of yang, and the moon is essence of yin. Master said that the utmost yang is the essence of the fire, and the the utmost yin is the essence of water, and the followers asked how fire comes from water, asked again to the master, how that is happened so. Master said that the universe was only created from water, so how we can say that the fire didn't come from water, and it could be said that there were only water of north pole before the creation of universe. The disciples questioned to the master, how we could talk that universe was created at the time of Ja[38]. Master said that it means water of the north pole of 1 and 6[39], and that we could say water is created by heaven. If think about this, it would be wonder whether water originated from the heaven or the heaven originated from water. To tell the truth, water bred the heaven and crossly, the heaven bred water, this mutual change of the universe could be a utmost alternation of the mysterious work of Hanullim[God].

---

[38]   Ja is the first word of the twelve terrestrial branches of eastern idea of a view of the world meaning birth, son, and second generation etc, the symbol animal is mouse./ writer

[39]   In korean, there is an idea of the native culture coming down from ancient era, generation to generation, it is that the directions have their own couple of numbers of 1 to 10, and their own images of five essences of water, tree, fire, soil, metal, as the alternate factors, for example, the north have the water essence with 1 and 6, the east have tree essence with 3 and 8, the south have fire essence with 2 and 7, the west have metal essence with 4 and 9, and the center have soil essence with 5 and 10. These directions have their own terrestrial animals, for example, north called Ja direction have the image of mouse, the beginning./writer

**   In this doctrine, we have to understand that the yin and yang theory of oriental thought is the momentum of the first origin of alternation in the universe like the electron and something getting opposite charge, as the term of water having **yin** image containing the **yang** image of hydrogen and helium atoms being origin of all materials in modern scientific view, "The north" is a word having image of direction only in case of plane, but if we think directions in the cosmos, there is directions as plane, so it would be better to understand the north as a beginning and creating area in the universe. Master Haewol had never learned modern science of chemistry and physics, but his speech of "Master said that the universe was only created from water, how we can't said that fire didn't come from water of itself, and so it could be said that there were only the water on the north pole before creation of universe." could be understood with the molecular chemistry that water molecule is composed of hydrogen and oxygen atoms which have strong firing specificity. And the hydrogen and helium atom which have the specificity of firing itself, might be very simple materials in the world, as well. /writer

Some followers questioned which is the former between the reason[truth] and the force[energy]. He answered, the heaven and earth, the yin and yang, the sun and moon and all the things alternated, and existed among the alternations of the reason[truth] and force[utmost energy]. And the greatest force could be understood with recognizing the heaven and earth, all works of Hanullim, and the all alternations originated from the utmost energy.

The nature of the transformation and the birth is belonging to the reason of heaven, and the nature of the movement and the alternation is belonging to the great force of heaven, accordingly the ghost[spirit] can not be seen, because it is anything of no shape and anything of no counting. The force[utmost energy] would not be comfortable but strong and sturdy, and the marvelous phenomenon [work of God] might be mysterious itself, if think their origin, it could be said that only the greatest force should be. The first one which formed force would be the reason, the movement after forming origin in force, and the reason become the force in the same time and in the same space, so it is impossible to divide them. If explain briefly the force[energy] is basically the origin of the work of God, and the reason is marvelous phenomenon of the work of God, and so the force breed the reason, at the same time the reason breed the force. Thus the heaven and the earth were formed as their regularity and fate, and all the things had got the reason which is truth of nothing no return as well, with this great truth the heaven and the earth is established and alternated.

7-2. Heaven and earth as father and mother

The heaven and earth are same as the father and mother, and the father and mother are same with the heaven and earth, and so, the heaven and earth become one, as the father and the mother become one. The mother's gestation with father can be thought as the gestation of earth with heaven. But nowadays human beings only know the reason of man's gestation except the reason of natures gestation. All lives living on the earth and below the heaven could have their life for the virtue of the heaven and earth, what we can say and how we can live except virtue of them. The sun and moon give us light and wind according to their character, what we can say this but the deepest thanks for them. The all natures are changed and generated to, so what can be called without the alternation of the greatest force and reason belonging to the heaven and earth. And so the heaven and earth can become the father and mother of all things in this world, in scriptures which the greatest Master Suwoon wrote, the term of Ju[sir, lord] was used after the word of Cheon[Heaven, God], in order to show our respect to the heaven and earth same as to our parent.[ref: nonhagmoon, main prayer of jumoon composed of 13 letters]

If think all, from antient era, though the all things have had been belonging to human beings' management, but it was said by the greatest Master Suwoon that we have to respect the heaven and earth, all natures, as well as we respect our parents. That doctrine to respect nature as parents, we men have had never heard those truth before our Master Suwoon, and I dare say the greatest Master Suwoon might create the new way for human beings to have to keep. Without this great virtue of doctrine, who could teach us that the truth of parents' relationship is the same with the nature and the cosmos? Please, not to forget the virtue to serve the heaven and earth always, you have to do it with deep heart, as if you should walk the road on the bluff with caution not to fall into the deep water, or on the thin ice surface of the deep river not to break, and with that way please serve the nature as your parents with devotion. If one would not respect one's parents, the parents become angry and punish severely their most lovely son or daughter, please don't forget this truth and take care of you.

Do we have to do the natural law serving our parents by the force of others? But we can meet some stupid men not to recognize that truth, because it is a reason for their misfortune not to get brightness, and for their laziness not to reach to the virtue without training mind, what a sorrowful it is for ourselves!

Human being is only one who can make super energy with the five essences of the cosmos, for alternation in the nature. The cereal crops are the original energy from the above five essences. As well the milk is the cereal of man, as the cereal become milk of nature for human beings. A gestation of the father and the mother is the same as a gestation of the heaven and the earth, and as well a baby sucks milk from the mom's breast, as a man sucks milk from the heaven and earth. As a baby growing up, he must take food of cereal, that is the milk of the heaven and earth, and so, by whom the milk and the cereals are given except the heaven and earth.

On knowing our birth and growth for parent's virtue, and on getting thought to thank to parents, one ought to have mind to serve one's parents, and on thinking virtue of heaven and earth, one have to thank for food every times to take food.[40] To pray of thanks every times for food is to feed back one's thankful mind for benignity of God, and to keep a vow not to forget virtue of the heaven and the earth as nature, the realities of Hanullim[God], that become the root of existence of mankind. How can we say that only human dress and take, without thinking that the sun dress and the moon take, as well. As well human cannot leave the heaven, as the heaven cannot leave human, and so, our one time of respiration, one time of movement, one time of dressing and one time of taking food become a frame to harmonize with others. They all breed human beings, and the heaven can work in the world by human beings, as well. More over, the actions of human beings, moving, dressing, eating are belonging to work of Hanullim[God]. And so, the frame of relationship between God and human being can never be broken, and leaved each other even just moment.

7-3. Other important doctrines of Master Haewol

7-3-1. Summary of the Way of Heaven [Dao]

The heaven and earth, the father and mother are different from each other when we read the terms, but if we think with insight, they are just a term of Heaven [Hanull]. To serve the heaven and the earth is the same as to serve parents. Generally, men make it important and valuable the thing that is seen only, but generally they disregard the things which is not visible. Please think

---

[40]   The most men who believe in God in the world, always pray to God with thanks for food, but it is hard for them to thank to each life sacrificed for men's food, for example, the cows changed to meat, the pigs changed to pork and ham, and many vegetables changed to salad. We have never called their name with thanks every times before taking food. In fact, in spite that we can't live without their lives, we have had lived without any thanks for them. If we would have some helps from policeman, whom do we give thanks to, the president or the policeman? We human beings have prayed with thanks like this way. If we feel thanks to them for preserving our life, it ought to call their name and give thanks though only one time in a month. If not, what a different manner is there between us and Incans, when we pray to God with thanks, except human sacrifice? /writer

twice and three times with insight, and you will recognize all things, and serve and revere them, and please practice with your best. Please search for the origin, recognize the origin, and you can recover the origin of your life. And you can understand the reason of the world, and you can be a cleverest one like a holy man in history. If Hanullim[God] do not give notice to any being, it become only a calm substance, they said this death and, if God take after one, we call him to be a spiritual one and they said this life, so, how we can not say that one's every movement is not belonging to Hanullim's order[God's order]. The husband and wife is the heaven and earth, so if the heaven and earth do not harmonize one another, Hanullim[God] don't like that, if they dislike each other she will punish them, if harmonized, they will be blessed.

7-3-2. To be none and to be real

Teacher's scripture said that mind can not be seen in nature, and if commune with one, no trace is found. In this nothing, spirit is there, so awareness can appear of itself. For the vessel being empty, all things can be put in it, for the house being empty, human can live in it For heaven and earth being empty, it can embrace all things. For mind being empty, one can commune with truth. After not to be, to be follow, after to be, it disappear again, so, nothing bear something, and something bear nothing. As well nothing bear something, as something is formed among the emptiness. It looks like nothing and emptiness, if try to look for, nothing can be found, and if try to listen, nothing can be heard.

Emptiness can bear energy, nothing can bear the reason, softness can make power, and strongness can grow energy, if not these four cases of alternation, no existence is possible in this world. If you make a trunk of mind with the energy of nothing and emptiness, and if you use the reason of nothing and emptiness, and when the spirit of emptiness reach to the truth, the silliness will disappear. The truth is the bearing reality among emptiness, that is the greatest virtue of heaven and earth, but the silliness come from the false of emptiness so it make the virtue of heaven none. If keep to the truth, you shall be loved by heaven [Hanullim:God], if silly, heaven will hate you. And so truth is the reality of life of heaven and earth, the false and silliness become a hammer to break human body. Something to be calm from emptiness, something to alternate from movement, and something to be formed from nothing, that is the truth of the only one greatest Energy[Hanullim:God]. Spirit to recognize, and spirit to be wise, is made by the reasonable energy among emptiness, if they gathered to form, it will be something, if they scattered to none, it will be nothing. for being right to be gathered, it can be, if to be lost to be scattered it can not be. If the reason and energy were right, it make all things spiritual, but if not, they are got disease. If the reason and energy of human body were right, it will be right the reason and energy of heaven and earth, if not, it will not be right

7-3-3. Mind spirit and holy spirit

Most men in the world didn't know that holy spirit of heaven[Hanullim:God] is amazing and miraculous. There are many men who believe in and pray to the big tree, the giant stone, the mountain, the ocean, and the several totems, the status and the symbol materials of religion as if there might be spirit, what a silly they are! Please listen to me and don't be foolish. Here I dare say in detail, think insight, recognize in bright, and please don't make sin to God. They said that the words of "mysterious phenomenon of Cosmos[work of God]", "ghost" "fate" "yin and yang", do you know the origin of "yin and yang"? After knowing the origin, you must say that you can understand Hanullim[God]. With what does the "yin and yang" formed? What does become the ghost? What does the fate come from? What does create the mysterious phenomenon of cosmos? And what does make the energy?

What does become the ghost? What does the energy become? If your mind controlling process reached to the filling state of listening without hearing with ears, and seeing without seeing with eyes, surely it could be said that you would reach to the state of complete stage of heaven's way, and you could recognize where and what such a miraculous phenomenon came from.

This doctrine means Hanullim's word to the Great Master Suwoon that "I become to succeed for meeting you now, though I have had tried but failed."

7-3-4. To serve men and things

As I said before, human being is thought to be a individual of natures of heaven, so serve man as we serve Heaven[God]. But many men do not have done this way. I have deplored that there are many men who have always been cockish for selfish mind, and I am afraid that somebody of them defect our Dao. To tell the truth, if I would, I could have such mind some times, but I did not, because I have deep anxiety for not to breed Hanullim's heart in my mind. If you have such a mind, where to and what for will you use it? One who would like to assume the air of someone, will be far from Dao, and if the other were true, it could be said that he will be near to Dao[truth]. They are not same each other, between one who knows it so, and one who believe it so, and one who feel it pleasure. One can be a someone who can do something for heaven and earth, after feeling good and pleasure. If somebody visit your home, please don't say that anybody comes, but say that Hanullim visit my home. If some woman learned Suwoon's doctrine beat the baby, the baby will die, so be careful not to beat babies and children. The virtue is base on humble. If somebody have lucidity and brightness, he might be wise enhough to know something as God, because the original heart of him having lucidity and brightness will make him do as Dao with it's best always. All that we have done every day must be Dao. If one become good, the world become good. According to one's gentleness, his home will be peaceful, and according to a home's peace, a country will become peaceful, and according to one country's peace, the world will become peaceful, who can repudiate it coming down as rain. Whenever you meet others, do as children do, and you will get your face in bloom, and you can harmonize with others and you can make a virtue. I have had learned something from everybody, so how can I say who can't be a teacher and who can't be a adult for me. Always I have had tried to learn something from a child and a woman, if it might be righteous.

As good carpenter doesn't deny the curved woods, and as a good doctor doesn't deny any patient, a good teacher doesn't deny anyone who want to learn. When you speak, think what you have done, and when you act, think what you have had spoken, if there is some differentiation between your word and your action, the heaven will depart from your mind, and then you will never become a holy man. Everything must have Heaven[The holy spirit:God:Hanullim], if one recognize this truth, he will never kill any life in the world though he was not taught not to kill the lives. After keeping small bird's eggs not to break, the beautiful larger birds will come and live in your garden, and after keeping used things without discard you will be rich. If you revere all things, your virtue will be spread all over the world.

7-3-5. Youngboo⁴¹ and Jumoon

[The figure of holy spirit and invocations for controlling mind]

The Mind (heart) is original nature in me as heaven, and so it could be said that all things of the heaven and earth have one mind originally. This mind is miraculous and spiritual, and the energy of heaven and earth is greatest wide and deep so it is full in the universe. In the doctrine written by Great Master show following sentence[ref: Podeokmun], "I have a **youngboo**[a figure of holy spirit] which is called **seonyak** [hanull's medicine]. It's shape is **taegeug**[oriental symbol of alternation based on **yin and yang**] ultimate of universe] and its form is also like **gung gung**[**gung** means bow and so gung gung is shape of two bows]. Please receive my youngboo of holy spirit and relieve humankind from disease with it. And receive also my jumoon [invocation] and teach people with them for me. And then, you shall have long life and the virtue of mine shall be spread out all over the world." In this sentence, geung-eul means the shape of mind. If your mind, and energy would be harmonized, you shall be harmonized with Heaven. [Hanullim: God] Most men try to heal their disease only with medication, because they don't know the reason why they can be treated by their mind control. Without controlling mind, to take drugs is to believe drugs not to believe Hanullim[God]. If mind were hurted by mind, disease should be happened by mind, if control mind with mind, the disease shall be healed by mind. If one know this reason of truth, and if he become a harmonized state of mind and energy, he might never take even a drop of water as a drug. This doctrine has a great sigficance of Hanullim's word to the Great Master that "I become succeed for meeting you now though I have had tried but failed."

Jumoon of three seven letters (21 letters) is heaven's letters drawing great Cosmos, Great Spirit, and great life. "**Shi-Cheon-Joo-Jo-Hwa-Jeong**" is the original root of alternation in this world and the birth of lives, and "**Young -Sae-Bool-Mang-Man-Sa-Jee**" is the original base of all to take. Human is born with holy spirit of Hanullim[God], and to live is to continue life with holy

---

⁴¹ Youngboo: A certain man translated youngboo to amulet or talisman, but it is not just same image of a figure of Holy spirit, so it might be in the right to call it "youngboo" as Korean called. / writer

spirit, but how we can tell that only human have spirit, all things in the heaven and on the earth have holy spirit, as well. And so, the true meaning of the way of our religion is that heaven breed heaven and heaven change heaven. The birth of all lives can be possible, after having this mind and energy, so through all in the universe, so all beings are connected each other with one energy and one mind.

7-3-6. To keep mind and energy righteously

If you can clear the wicked from the original mind, and if you can make the ocean of energy in you clean, and if you keep your mind not to be contaminated by all dirties of greed, the spirit of heaven and earth shall come back to your body. If one's mind would not be clean and bright he becomes silly, and if one would be, one becomes clever like a holy man.

The body is a home of spirit and the spirit is owner of body, to be spirit in your body means to be good and comfortable, but to be greedy means not to be good and not to be comfortable. The spirit is only heaven [Hanullim:God] so it is the highest one with endlessness, the widest one with extremeness, and the greatest vigor, and the greatest valor. If work in our body, one shall be bright and clever, if treat things, one shall be respectful. If recognize it, one can get the reason of heaven, because a thought is belong to the spirit originally, not to the sensory organs of body. To keep mind and energy righteous is to connect again the broken fate to heaven and earth. If the nature stay at the center of your body, you must feel comfortable, and if the spirit reach to the center of your body, all will be known naturally.

7-3-7. Sincerity, reverence and faith

The doctrines of Donghak religion can be identified with only three word of sincerity, reverence and faith. It is very hard to practice them without great virtue, so if one made it easy, one become holy man easily just as putting hand up side down. Sincerity is the way of action not to stop and not to change, this is the same as the way of heaven and earth, if one did so, he can be called a great holy man.

If some one reverent one's mind he must become great comfortable and harmonized, if some body reverent others, many a man will be gathered around him, if some body reverent all the things the natures will come to him, gloria! to reverent and to reverent! It is only great one energy to be full in the universe, it is hard to walk even a step without caution. Please think the earth as well as the skin of your mother. Which is more important mother's skin or your stockings? If one know this truth and practice with reverent mind, he might never wet even in the heavy raining.

Not to be faith to man is same as not to be vehicles to carriage, and the faith could never borrowed by family. To believe in mind is to believe in Haullim[God] and to believe in Hanullim[God] is to believe in mind, so if any one didn't have faith, he must be not only but a storage of foods. First of all, faith is essential for trainig mind, and if one would have faith, sincerity and reverence is followed in nature.

7-3-8. To train mind hardly

If one would train mind hardly, there is nothing not to succeed. Think of heaven's way always as some foods needed when you are hungry, as some clothes needed when you are cold, and as water needed when you are thirsty. Can the rich only train mind? Can the ruler only train mind? Though they are poor and lower, the all p[eople can control their mind. Learn widely, question in detail, and practice hard with sincerity. If you would not understand the heaven's way, and not be bright and spiritual, those must be the reason why you didn't have sincerity and faith. Don't have greedy, don't have things and honor for selfish and than the energy and spirit shall be gathered in you, so you shall get wisdom to understand all in bright.

7-3-9. The way how to train mind.

It is not good only to invoke to commune with spirit without thought of truth, and it is in the wrong to study the reason of heaven's way without invocation. Please don't forget that the two ways of training mind have done together. If I think heaven, and the heaven think me at the same time, so I and heaven must become one. But if my energy would not be in the right and my mind would move, it become out of heaven's order. If my energy would be in the right and my mind would be fixed, it become one with the virtue of heaven. To succeed or not is belong to the state of one's mind and energy which are righteous or not. Please train my mind, not to ask for far, and please think again in order that I am keeping my mind bright and pure, without breach.

7-3-10. Three kind of reverence

At first, human have to reverent heaven, that was taught only by our Great Master. One who don't know the reason to reverent heaven is one who can not love truth, because heaven is the center of truth. To reverent heaven do not mean to reverent some existence in the sky, but to reverent my mind in me. It is the way to know that to reverent my mind become to reverent heaven[Hanullim:God], so not to reverent my mind is not to reverent the heaven and earth. When one reverent heaven, he can know his eternal life and the truth that all things are equal, and so one can have mind to sacrifice for others and to do his duty for the world. At last to reverent heaven is the way to get the center of all truth in one's hand. Second, human have to reverent people each other, to reverent heaven become to appear to the real when one reverent man. If one reverent heaven without reverence for people, it is the same that one might hope to have grain without sowing the seeds. One, who hope to train mind, have to serve a man as one serve for Hanullim, become one who practise the Dao in the right. If somebody come to your home, please don't say that a man comes, but Hanullim[God] comes. Hanullim is in all creatures by due, it is the same that one reverent Haullim[God] without reverence for human being, as that one hope to quench his thirst after spilling water out. Third is to reverent materials. Human being can not reach to the highest state of virtue, only with that the human reverent each other. One can be said that he have the highest virtue to harmonize with the heaven and earth, as long as he can have the mind to reverent materials.

7-3-11. Hanullim feed on Hanullim

Every times I preached sermon that all things are Hanul and all works are Hanul. If one accepted this truth, there is the relationship of "Hanul feed on Hanul." In a certain point of view, it can be hard to understand, but if we think all in the universe, in case of same quality of energies, Hanul make them help each other for being constant state, and in case of different quality, Hanul make them feed on each other for harmonized natural state.

So with this energizing way, we can understand that Hanul breed[maintain] the species[materials] in order to make each different energy to be harmonized. Accordingly, the image of "Hanull feed on Hanull" can be understood as a universal method for communication and alternation of energy, and so, the utmost amazing rule of heaven only belongs to the law of harmonization of the great energy of universe.

8

Introduction of Doctrines of Suwoon [Donggyungdaejon][42]

8-1. Podeokmun [Doctrine on propagating virtue]

From ancient era, the four seasons of spring, summer, autumn, and winter have rotated regularly. The exchanges of seasons have been repeating orderly fashion without any irregularity. In this natural environment, humankind and all beings have had lived, This order of seasons, and the order of nature, is the traces of alternation of Hanullim[God][43] by whom all things were created. But the ignorant people did not know that Hanullim[God] sent rain and dew, by which all things have had been renewed and have had grown. But they only thought that all things began and developed naturally without original reason. In ancient times, they thought there were virtuous kings, who made wise laws and ruled the people with compassion and justice. Thereafter, sages were born and they interpreted the movement of the sun, moon, and stars, and they made a calendar and writings of astronomy. Then, they determined the unchanging

---

[42]   Cheondogyo scripture, University press of America, Inc. translated to English by Young Choon Kim and Suk San Yoon, 2007. The original scriptures were written by Great Master Suwoon by himself after getting experience to meet with deity.

[43]   The word Hanullim is composed of two parts, hanul means the image of the greatest spherical shaped cosmos with outer border, and '-nim(-lim)' is a suffix meaning reverence, so Hanullim, attached lim of suffix to the simple mechanical noun hanul meaning great sphere, become getting personality in Korean language. For example, if we could use 'waternim ', water is getting image of personality like human being. And so, the word 'Hanullim' is same meaning the word of 'God'.

nature of the natural law, and they taught people that the mind and action of humankind, as well as, all the changes of the universe depended on the will of Hanullim. The sages had reverence for the will of Hanullim and followed the principle of Hanullim.

The people who respected the will of Hanullim and followed the principle of Hanullim became the excellent, and through their learning, they attained a high level of moral virtue. The way that they followed is called as the way of Hanul[Heaven] and the virtue that they cultivated is called as the Hanullim's virtue. People of ancient era who had been enlightened by the Hanul's Way[the way of heaven] and had cultivated virtue, became the excellent, and futhermore, some of them became great sages. Isn't it a wonderful and joyful event?! However, in recent era the people have a selfish mind, and do not follow the principle of Hanul[Heaven] nor care for the will of Hanullim[God]. Therefore, my mind is always anxious and fearful, so I don't get to know what will happen in future. In 1860 there were rumors that the Westerners were not seeking for wealth or glory, but serving with God's will, yet they attacked and conquered other countries of the east, and built their churches and spread their religion. I wonder whether it was the true reason for their invasion, or they were motivated by other means.

In April, suddenly I felt chilling without any other abnormality, like common cold, so I did not know exactly what was wrong, and I just could not describe such a feeling happened to me. Then, suddenly, a mysterious voice came to listen and it made me scared and surprised, and on searching around I asked, "Who are you? Is any body here?"

But the voice only said: "Please don't fear and don't be afraid of me, your people call me Hanullim [God]; don't you recognize Hanullim?"

I asked him "Why do you reveal yourself to me?" and Hanullim said: "I can not search for anyone to teach people the truth. Thus, I am sending you to the world to teach people the truth, and therefore, never doubt me."

I asked him, Hanullim, "Do you want that I shall teach them the western [christian: catholic] doctrine of God?" and then he said, "No, I have a yeongboo[figure of holy spirit] which is called seonyak[mystical medicine]. Its shape is taegeuk[symbol of the great ultimate of universe, which composed of yin and yang, eg. central circle of Korean flag] and its form is also like gung gung[gung means bow and so gung gung is the shape of two bows], as well. Please receive my yeongboo of holy spirit and with it cure humankind's disease.

Also, receive my jumoon[invocation] and teach people it for me. Then, you shall have long life and the virtue of mine shall be spread out all over the world."

After communication with Hanullim and hearing the words of him, I drew the yeongboo of spirit on a piece of paper [called Korean paper which is made from Edgeworthia chrysantha Lindl without any chemical reagent] and burned it on a dish, mixed it with water, and swallowed it. Then suddenly I felt healthy and some uncomfortable syndrome of my body vanished, and so I came to realize that the seonyak[mystical medicine] was responsible. When I applied it to the illnesses of other people, some were cured, but others were not. I wondered about the reason for this phenomenon and watched carefully and found out that, sincere and true believers who honored Hanullim received positive results, but to those who disobeyed the truth and disregarded virtue of Hanullim, received no effect at all. Therefore, isn't it all based on the sincerity and reverence of th recipient's mind? Recently, the people have to live without comfort, because our country has been filled with the bad environment, this is an indication of the bad fortune of our nation. The Western powers are victorious every time they fight, and takeover wherever they attack, there seems to be nothing that they cannot achieve. I am worried that if China is destroyed, Korea may be next. where can we find a way supporting our nation and comforting the people? Alas! The people of this generation do not understand that a new era is coming. Most men hearing my words didn't believe and denied what I said, more over out of the door, they gossiped about my teaching. Thus, they do not follow the truth and virtue of Hanullim, these are truly worrisome to me.

Even the wise men would believe rumor that my doctrine might have been false; it is regrettable and sorrowful to me that I become not to convince anyone in the world. And so I am writing this [Podeokmun] to instruct people. Receive this writings with respect and admire my teaching always.

8-2. Nonhakmun [A discussion on Truth]

The Hanull[the way of heaven] is formless but has traces. The Earth is vast and great, yet it has directions. The Hanull has the nine stars[44] and likewise

---

[44]   'Nine' is hard to identify, some said from oriental story, but I can't agree, I suggest that the word of nine might mean the number of recreation of cosmos.

the Earth has the nine provinces. The Earth also has eight directions which correspond to the eight trigrams. Thus, the universe consists of the numbers and principles according to which waxing, waning, and exchanging appeared in turn, but there is no truth of movement, quietness, change, and alternation of itself. Among the myriad things in the universe which are produced through the interplay of yin and yang, humans alone are the most spiritual beings.

Thus, the principle of three essentials (heaven, earth, and human beings) is established, and from which the number of the five elements was produced. What are the relations of the five elements? Heaven is the frame of the five elements, the earth is the material of the five elements, and humankind is the vital energy of the five elements.[45] Therefore, we can understand that heaven, earth, and human are constituted to the essentials on this world.

The four seasons rotate without a change of order, and wind, dew, frost, and snow appear in a timely manner. Many people, who are like dews, do not understand the reasons for it. Some people say that it is God's grace, and others say that it is the work of nature. However, even though some people say that it is the grace of God, it cannot be shown, and even though others say that it is the work of nature, it is difficult to prove. Thus, from the ancient to the present, people have not had known exactly the real reason for it.

In April 1860 the country was in chaos, accordingly most people's minds were confused, and no way and no solution was known. More over strange rumors were rampant countrywide: the Westerners had realized truth and virtue, and through their inventions they can accomplish anything. If they attack with their weapons, no one can withstand them. If China were destroyed, wouldn't Korea face the same fate? They said the westerners had the doctrine which is called Catholicism or the holy religion. Did they know the time of Heaven was upon us? Or did they receive any mandate from God?

When I considered each of these questions, I had to be anxious, and regreted only late birth of me. At this time, suddenly my body became shook, and I felt sensitized with a certain force through my entire body, and inwardly

---

[45]   the five elements: the eastern world view that all the alternation in the universe is based on the five vital circular changes of direction according with the image of he five primary substances of metal, wood, water, fire, and soil, not to mean just material itself but imagination.

I heard divine words of instruction. I was surprised and looked around but no one could be found. I listened clearly but could not hear anything with my ears. Therefore, I felt it very strange because I had never had such an experience and so after bracing and controlling my mind and renewing my energy, I asked, "What did happen to me?"

Then, a clear answer could be listen, "My mind is your mind. How can humankind know me? People can see only the sky and the earth, but they do not know Spirit is real. Human beings only know the spirit called ghost, it's me, too. I am just the Spirit of Divine. Now I am giving you the everlasting, limitless truth, and so cultivate and refine it, write it down and teach people with it. Establish the laws of practice and propagate the truth of virtue. Then the world shall be brightened and you shall have long life." For almost a year I practiced and contemplated the truth, and then I realized that it is none other than the principle of nature. Therefore, I composed the jumoon[invocation], and looked for the way on how to receive the spirit, Hanullim, and I wrote a poem of "not to forget Hanullim." All the ways of practicing truth and controlling mind are addressed in the twenty one letters of jumoon.

In 1861, year after communication with God, intelligent scholars came to see me from all around provinces of the country and asked, "They said that the spirit of God came down on you, what happened to you Master? Please teach us." I replied, "I received the truth of 'nothing of no return' in the universe." They asked, "And what did you call the truth?" I replied, "It is the righteous Dao[way]." They asked, "What is the difference from the Western way?" I answered, "The western religion [Christianity] is similar, but a little different. Their prayer has no reality but both have the same destiny, and their way to God is identical, and so their doctrines of truth are taught differently by their church."

They asked "Why is that so?" I answered, "Our way is the natural way. If each person preserves a good mind, rectifies the vital force, follows their original nature, and they can receive the wisdom of divine, and all that will turn out well naturally.[called moowee-ihwa*] The westerners have no order in their words and no logic in their writings. There is no genuine service for God, but they only pray for selfish ideas. Therefore, they do not have the mystical experience of uniting with the spiritual force, and they lack the true teaching of God. Their religion has form but no reality. They have vague ideas but no real invocation. Their religion is close to emptiness and their doctrine is not really for God. Therefore, how can one say that there is no difference between the western religion and my teaching?"

They asked, "You said that the way is identical; then, could we call your way western worship?" I replied, "No, I was born in the east, and I received the call from God in the east. Therefore, although the way is called the righteous way, the learning is called Donghak [eastern doctrine] as the world is divided to the east and the west, and how can the west be called the east and the east be called the west? Confucius was born at the small country of Lu and taught in Tsou, therefore, his teaching is called the school of Tsou-Lu and spread throughout the world. Likewise, I received the way in this land [Korea] and spread it from this country, and so how can my doctrine be called western learning?"

They asked, "What are the meanings of the jumoon?" I answered, "The jumoons are words which honour Hanullim with the utmost sincerity, reverence and faith, which in our words means utmost love. There are jumoons today as well in the ancient times. They asked, "What is the meaning of the jumoon of Ji-Gi-Geum-Ji-Weon-Wee-Dae-Gang which prays for the Spirits to come down?" I answered: "The Ji means the highest, greatest and utmost, the Gi means the vital force and energy with holy spirit which is vast and full in the universe, and so the Ji-Gi is the mysterious utmost Energy and Holy Spirit which touches and governs all things in the cosmos. It is hard to describe exactly to be understood in a word. It seems to be sound, and it can be listen, but not seen. Geum-Ji means that one wants to be joined with the Holy Spirit and unified with the vital force of the Great Universe, Weon-Wee means hoping to be and praying to be, Dae-Gang means that the ultimate energy is coming down on me and the hope to be united with it.

Another main jumoon which formed thirteen letters of Shi-Cheon-Ju-Jo-Hwa-Jeong, Young-Shae-Bul-Mang-Man-Sa-Ji. Shi means having the divine spirit within and expressing the vital force of life. When people realize this truth, they will keep it in their hearts without movement. Cheon means Hanullim[God], and Ju refers to respecting, honoring, and serving God like one's own parents. Jo-Hwa means natural alternation and transformation without any intentional interference. Jeong means oneness with the divine virtue and deciding to have the spiritual mind of Hanullim[God]. Young-Shae refers to the long life of humankind. Bul-Mang means thinking about Hanullim always never forgetting. Man-Sa means numerous things. Ji means understanding God's way and achieving wisdom. Thus, if one would think about and never forget the bright truth and virtue of God with the jumoon of 21 words, the man will unite with the ultimate spirit and energy of Hanullim[Ji-Gi] and attain the perfect sage hood. The disciples asked, "If the mind of Hanullim is identical with the mind of humans, why is there good and evil?" I answered: "Hanullim ordains the reason of high and low qualities of life, and he determines the principles of joy and sorrow. The virtues of the excellent are originated to the righteous energy [vital force] and a stable mind, and therefore, his virtue is one with the virtue of the universe. But the stupid has wrong energy and an unstable mind and therefore violates the will of God. Isn't this the principles of success and failure?"

The disciples asked, "Why don't the people of the world revere God?" I answered: "To call out God when they are facing death is the common inclination of human beings. The ancient sages said that the destiny of human beings were determined by God's will, because God created all humankind, such sayings remained to be valid even today. However, the most peoples of this world do not revere God, because they do not recognize exactly whether God exist or not. The disciples asked, "Why do some people disparage your teaching?" I answered, "Sometimes it can happen." They asked, "How is it possible?" I replied: "Because my way is the truth which one has never heard in the past so far, and it is incomparable to any doctrine in the present or in the past. Cultivating and practicing my way might be heard to be futile, but it has a real and positive result, while merely listening is futile, although it may have the appearance of some result. The disciples asked, "Why do some people betray your way and turn away from it?" I answered, "It is not even worth of discussing them." They asked, "Why don't they be worth of talking about?" I answered: "By distancing from them, you avoid harm." They asked, "What was their minds when they came in, and what was their minds when they left?" I answered: "Their minds are shaky like grass over which the wind blows." They asked, "Then, how can those people receive the spirit?" I answered: "God's spirit is given whether they are good or bad." They asked, "Is there misfortune to them?" I replied: "In the ancient times of the reign of the benevolent kings, the people were good like virtuous kings. The destiny of this world is the same direction following to the world. Their fortune is belonging to the hands of God not in my power. As we investigate each one, we do not know clearly what kind of future they will have, and we cannot talk about their destiny whether they will have good fortune or not, so it is neither what you should ask for nor my duty to answer for."

Amazing! How brilliant your questions of God's way are! If my crude description may not enough to convey the deep and righteous essentials of truth, but there can not be any doubt to correct immorality, to cultivate humanity, to develop potential, and to restore righteous mind. The infinite truth of cosmos and earth, and the ultimate principle of the way are all contained in these work. Receive this writings respectfully and help to spread the holy truth of God. On comparing with that, it might be the taste which can be harmonized by sweetness, and the whiteness which can be absorbed all the colors. Now the way of heaven appreciated me and the joy of acknowledge is overwhelming. Thus, on teaching and showing this truth to you, study it carefully and clearly, and never lose the profound opportunity provided by Hanullim[God].

8-3. **Sudeokmun** [On cultivating virtue]

To be born, to be grown, to bear fruit, and to harvest is the constant way of cosmos. To obey and to follow to the constant way of cosmos with pure mind is the proper conduct of humankind. To know all these, originated to the sages of old era, and to the knowledge of the former scholars. Although the knowledge might be shallow and insignificant, it must be gain through the virtuous teaching of the former scholars. I was born in the East, and only spending times and days only for studying Confucianism without farming, and barely preserving my family name, and unable to escape the environment of a poor scholar. My ancestors' loyalty and uprightness to the King was left in small mountain Yongsan. In accordance with the virtue of our King, the year of 1592[46] and the year of 1636[47] returned.

Thus the virtue of my ancestors has flown down without interruption through the era. Father was a honorous scholar of philosophy of Chinese and

---

[46]   The year when his grand father was a general to fight against the small men of Jap's invasion.

[47]   The year when his grand father was a general to fight against the soldiers of Mongol's invasion.

Korean, and this familiar honor has been flown down, over the six generations, what a glorious this familiar history to me as a descendants!

But Alas! What a corrupt political system of the monarchism of the last Chosun dynasty![48] At last, my father's hope as a scholar was blown out like a transient spring dream. All of his efforts and desires toward a good governor for poor peoples became useless. After those times, he had done only composition poems and he got to live with the idea of naturalism, at small pavilion named Yongdamjeong which was built in the valley of the Gumi Mountain by himself. As the flowing time cannot be stopped, one day my father passed away as the beautiful stream of Yongchu flow down away, and so I was sunk down deeply into the sorrow pond, and left alone at the age of sixteen on this rough world. How I could know other job except studying, since I was grown only with learning books of Confucius with late father. More over, the firing accident of straw roofing house took all of the books, works, the writings of my father's away to be perished without trace, and there became full in my heart with sadness as his only son. What a sorrowful accident to me! I needed to work and wanted to support my family, but I did not know how to agriculture. Since the assets of my family had gradually decreased, I was afraid what might happen in the future. Becoming adult and getting age more, I lamented for hard fate of my life.

As I contemplated my destiny, I feared the possibility of coldness and hunger of my family. Though over forty age, I did not have a definite place to live, who could say that the earth was wide and big? As all things that I did, became nothing, I lamented the difficulty of finding a small place to live. From this time, I shook off the Confucianism and anxiety of this world, and cast aside that which entangled my heart. The old house at Yongdam, my home town was the place, wherein my father had gained respect from many scholars who lived near Kyuongjoo area for his great scholarly knowledge of Confucianism, and which had been the capital of ancient country, Shilla for 1000 years. On October, 1859 I came back home, to the old house with my wife and children, And on April 1860, I received the revelation of the truth from Hanullim[God]. It was an event like a dream, and it was an mysterious experience that was difficult to describe with words. After that time I had studied again with the old book of eight trigrams for divination, I realized that

---

[48]   At that times, the corrup officers used to sail the official position with big money

the rulers in prehistoric times had followed to the will of Heaven, but after that times they didn't.

With sincere heart, I had trained my mind according to the way that Hanullim showed me, and I found that the truth is not different from the law of nature. If think with Confucianism, it is similar to heaven's way [Dao], but somewhat different. As all doubt was brushed out, I became confident to realize it with that the doctrine given by Hanullim on April in 1860 is the universal truth, and just the ethical truth for all humankind.

For a while, with putting aside the idea to devote my life for propagating the truth, and offered a devout prayer earnestly, thus, I delayed to propagate truth. The year of 1861 came, after June, many peoples who concerned my new doctrine came to be full in my house. And so I had to organize them for controlling mind. Some wise man hoping to participate in the studying my doctrine and inquiring interpetation about the way of truth, I solicited them to propagate my word countrywide. In my heart I had the elixir of life, its shape look like **gung-eul**.[49] The **jumoons** to recite are only 3, 7 letters[50]. As I opened the door and welcomed guests, their numbers became large, and I prepared the training hall with great joy. The scenes of many followers listening to me with polite attitude, and the scenes of the children bowing with polite manner, and the sound of their recitation of **Jumoon**[invocation] gave me a great pleasure. Some of adults being older than me, looked like followers of Confucius's. Humaneness, righteousness, propriety, and wisdom, are virtues taught by the former sages

But keeping a good mind and having the right spiritual force are the virtues established only by me. The initiation ceremony is a solemn vow of religion to serve hanullim forever. To remove all doubts is to keep sincerity. And to wear one's clothes and hat correctly is the well manner of the noble man. To eat on the road and to hold hands behind one's back are acts of the mean-spirited fellow. At home of my followers, don't take bad meat of four legs animal[now days, the followers think this animal to be dog]. and don't sit

---

[49] gung-eul means the arc and bird shape, same as the shape of taegeug

[50] twenty one letters, such expression originated to Korean custom. Usually the most Korean express the numbers with 7multiple, when they said about life. For example, they said the early stage of infant's life with 7, 2x7, 3x7 days, and they think the man's spirit will stay for 7x7 days on the earth after his death.

suddenly in cold water. To take the freedom of married women is forbidden by the law of the dynasty, and to recite the **Jumoon** with a loud voice while in bed is lazy behavior to the hanul's way, therefore I declare these teachings become the rules of life. How beautiful our way is! Those who follow to our way are able to write as beautifully as a famous calligrapher, and they are able to sing beautiful songs, even though they may be low class laborers. Those who follow our way and repent of their past mistakes do not desire the wealth of the millionaire, and those who have the sincerity for our way, and who do not envy the intellect of genius. The appearance of believers change and become to the mystic sages, and their bright faces after getting well from chronic disease are enough to forget the names of famous doctors.

However, in order to fulfill the way of hanul and to establish virtue of Hanullim, the success depend on one's genuine sincerity and one's character. If somebody controlled his mind as well the way as they learn by rumors, and some person recited the **jumoon** as such way, what a wrong behavior and what a cringe worthy manners are! I am very anxious and fear that the splendid and glorious virtue of Hanullim's must be misunderstood by them. But all the reason of their mistake is due to my absent where my followers study[51], knowing the minds of us can correspond with each other though there are far distance between us, but my passion of longing can not be suppressed, therefore, I write and show this to all of followers, so please take notice of my words. In our religion, the sincerity is to believe in with unaffected heart. Among the words they said, some are true and some are false. Choice true words, and reject false words, and then thinks again and decide firmly. Faith is not to believe all words, but to firm up decision which you made. And if one would practice in such a way, he will achieve the sincerity. The principles of sincerity and faith are not so far apart. And the word sincerity is composed of word and achievement.[52] Thus, if you have faith, and then sincerity is sure to follow. Here I teach you unambiguously.

---

[51]   At this time, he stayed at solitary small temple like house to keep off misfortune to be arrested for being entrapped by Confucius's in that society of dynasty

[52]   This sentence means the figure of old Korean hieroglyphic letter[so called Chinese letter] of sincerlity, which formed with two parts of meaning word and meaning achievment. Aren't they believable words? With the mind of reverence and sincerity, please do not renege on my words of instruction.

8-4. Buryeon-giyeon [Not so, yet so]

As the old song, all things of thousand years ago, was formed and had unique features. When we talk about what we see, it might be said so so, but if we could determine their origins, there are very far from those which we recognize and determine and describe. When we think about our parent's life, we are aware that our parents preceded us, and when we think about our future, we are aware that our descendants will be continuous through successive generations. And when we think sbout our future again, its principle does not differ from our thought about our present's life. However, when we consider past generations, one question arise in our mind, and we can find that it is difficult to understand how the first parents of humankind became human beings. Ah! such a thought to account the origin! When we consider obvious things, we find them easy to understand and we can say so, but when we think more over than that times, it is very difficult to understand, and only we can say not so. How is it so? How did the first leader of mankind become a king? Since we can't know his origin, how can anyone not regard this as a strange? In this world, no one can exist without parents, therefore, when we consider the ancestors of us, we cannot but say so and so. And so, only we can say that, for the benefit of the world, Kings and teachers must appeared. Kings should rule by law and teachers instruct with propriety. The first King in the world had no previous King whom he succeeded from, how did he receive the code of law? Since the first teacher in the world had no predecessor who instructed him, from whom could he learn propriety and righteousness? These are indeed an unknowable things. Did all these events happen, because such leaders had knowledge from the moment of their birth, or because their knowledge developed by themselves naturally on growing? Even if one says that they had knowledge from the time of birth, at that stage our mind are still in darkness, and even if one says that all their knowledge was developed by themselves, the truth is far away and hard to reach for us to understand.

Because we do not know the reason why certain things came to be so, and we cannot explain them, only we can say not so. And because we also know why certain things are so, we can affirm and maintain them, so we can say so.

Therefore, if we assess the alpha and omega of all things, how far from the great principle that the formed become the formed and the truth become the truth is! Why people do not know that? Why people do not know that? How many years have had gone after determining the order of universe? The destiny of universe come and recover by itself. Never has it had changed through all ages! How could we say about the destiny and recovery? All things in the world is thought not so, and I will consider, clarify, write, and reflect on them here.

There is order in the four seasons. why is it so? Really, why is it so? There is water on the top of mountains. How is it so? Really, how is it so? A little baby knows their parents even though they cannot speak and recognize. Thus, why don't the people of this world know the holy man's birth? The cow that listen to their masters' words and cultivate the farms, seems to have mind and recognize. These cow have been forced to work and lived for their master. Then, why do they suffer and die for man? Do they know filial piety and love? Swallows might know their masters. No matter poor their masters may be, they return to their old nest under the small straw thatched roof every year. Therefore, those things which are easy to determine must be said so, and if not, it can be said not so. If we search for the far origin of all things, they can be said not so, not so, and not so. But if we consider that the all beings must originate to the Creator, they can be said so, and this is the truth of existence of all things in the world.

8-5. Chukmoon [Main Prayer]

I deeply appreciate that I was born in America [the name of the prayer's country] as a human being with the best spirituality, and that I have received the blessings bestowed on me by the heaven and earth. But so far, I had not realized the way to the truth, by way of sinking in deep suffering ocean of impure mind. Now In this holy world, I meet a great Master and I can realize the truth, and I repent deeply the past faults. I want to do only all the good and never forget the Master's doctrine eternally. Here I get to know that controlling mind is the way to God, and I will train my mind as the way Master showed. On a good today, after cleaning this place, I am praying with my best sincerities and with my best wishes, please commune with me.

8-6. Two Jumoons [Invocations]

A) Gangryung jumoon [Invocation for holy spirit's coming down]
    Ji-Gi-Geum-Ji-Won-Wee-Dae-Gang*[53]

B) Bon Jumoon [The main invocation]
    Shi-Cheon-Ju-Jo-Hwa-Jeong-yeong-Shae-Bool-Mang-Man-Sha-Ji[54]

8-7. Gangshi [The poem given by God]

Do-Rae-3-7-Ja, Hang-Jin-Sae-Gan-Ma[55]

8-8. JwaJam [Proverbs]

My doctrine is great spacious but simple, and can be explained not with many words but only three words, sincerity, reverence and faith. After training mind with these, you can get to be enlightenment at last, and so don't be afraid to be distracting mind, but be afraid only not to reach to the knowledgement of truth.

8-9. Jeonpaljul [Eight verses, written first]

A) If you don't know where the brightness of God is, don't look for it out side of you but training your mind.
B) If you don't know where the virtue of God is, think that how your body get life.

---

[53]   This invocation means that praying for the ultimate energy and the holy spirit to come down.

[54]   This invocation means that I believe that I have Hanullim[God]in me (as the state of the holy spirit being enshrined in my body, and the vital power being energized from outside of my body.) and that Hanullim make me fixed to the harmony of alternation, not to forget the truth forever but to be wise with the spirit of the Creator.

[55]   This poem means that on drawing 21 letters, all the evil of the world surrender out.

C) If you don't know where the order of God, consider your mind to be utmost brightness.

D) If you don't know where the way of God is, account your faith is only one.

E) If you don't know whether the sincerity of God is, fathom your mind is lost.

F) If you don't know what the reverence of God do, don't relax to adore.

G) If you don't know what the awe do, consider yourself to be utmost fair without selfish.

H) If you don't know whether your mind loss, observe whether you mix the public and the private.

8-10. Hoopaljul [Eight verses, written later]

A) If you don't know where the brightness of God is, send your mind there.

B) If you don't know where the virtue of God is, it's hard to say too vast.

C) If you don't know where the order of God is, it's mysterious truth to give and take.

D) If you don't know where the way of God is, no others but to take care of yourself.

E) If you don't know whether the sincerity of God is, know your laziness of yourself.

F) If you don't know what the reverences of God do, fear yourself not to recognize your ignorance.

G) If you don't know what the awe do, act as sinner at the place of no sin.

H) If you don't know whether your mind loss, think your last mistake.

9

Introduction of Cheonboogyung*

-the scripture of heaven

Cheonbugyung was discovered in the state of 81 hieroglyphic letters* written on the tortoiseshell which was passed down from kingdom of ancient era of old Korea, which had been prosperous before 3000-4000 years B.C. in the north east Asia. It was very hard to translate to English, because there were no relational terms between word to word, so in Korea there are several opinions to interpret them and to translate to modern Cheonboogyung, significance.

In brief, it might be showed the reason of creation of universe and alternation of birth, growth, prosperity and declination with the numbers of 1 to 9. Cheonboogyung is the oldest doctrine coming down to Korean people from the first leader of ancient country, Geobalhan I [King of Geobal I: BC 3898-3805]. He came down to the Taebaeg mountain area of earth from universe, and made a village called Shinsi with his followers of big group. Than he requested to a follower named Hyukduk to write this doctrine and to preserve it to hand down to his descendants. To understand this mythological doctrine to be real coming down to recent era, here we have to know ancient Korean people's history that when and where they came from. Most scholars who have researched ancient history of Korean maintain their opinion that ancient Korean people might move from central north area near Baikal Lake and Ural-Altai mountains, and that they would have earlier age of bronze and iron ware than others because there were many stones containing metals around the river and lake where they lived. When they moved to north side of east Asia through Mongolia or Amur river of north east area, they might have excellent cultivation of bronze and iron ware, because there were many river side stones which contained iron materials. About this historical fact is seen in the History book of Han, unified old China's name which was written by Samacheon, a historian lived about 100 years B.C. who is famous historian of the old Han country built by Yoobang, leader of the Hwaha peoples(name of old Chinese lived upper-center area of Yellow river). And he wrote about some special man named Shinnong who teached Hwaha peoples agricultural technique was a first Governer dispathed from old Korean people's country. [Nowdays he had been worshiped as a God of cultivation among the Chinese] with his book, we can find the first combat between Korean people and Hwaha people at the battle called Panlok (means wide green plain) and the leader of Hwaha peoples, Kongson (surname, later he became the old chinese king named Heonwon) was defeated by Mr.Chiwoo, general of Korean peoples, and the reason of this fight was a accident of killing their Governer Shinnong whom most Chinese have thought to be their God of agriculture for Mr. Kongson's act of treachery. And another interesting sentence about Chiwoo who weared iron mask for fight was the monster with iron headed being. Samacheon said this accident was happened about the times of BC 1000-2000. This war was ought to give the victory to General Chiwoo. About Chiwoo, ther was a interesting sentences written by Samacheon, that Chiwoo was not a man but a having a grotesque face and body with four legs, to Hwaha people it migh be a amaging stranger who weared iron mask and a protect instrument for horse. Even though he wrote what he heard from premitive peoples who lived old panlok area, we can know the difference of cultivation between old Korean and old Chinese through these records which Samacheon wrote. After this Panlok war, as all the ancient warfare so, the side of large population could be hold a prominent position to opposite, more over with the modified instrument with iron and bronze, the next war between two peoples, King

Chiwoo (after Panlok battle, he became King of Korean peoplets) defeated and so after this Panlok battle, Korean people have had to keep their country losing their ancient territory of Yellow river area known with old civilization of Yellow river area. And after Han era of old China had invaded the north area from Baijing to Manchuria with great number of soldiers. If China accepted to excavate the ruins of an ancient city of Yellow river culture suspected area under drifted soil layer at the down stream areas of Yellow river, and ancient cultural heritage site of Hongsan [Red mountains] area situated east side of Manchuria with UN or Korea together, and than world citizens can find out some evidence of old Korean's cultivation. More over the most citizens of world do not know that old Korean language had influenced to the language of east asia people of old Chinese and Sumerian. Due to the reason for small population, Korean have had tragic history of invasion by big countries of old China and old Mongolia, every times of their invasion they always destroyed all of our historical evidence of culture and civilization. Unfortunately, in recent era, undeveloped country of Japan, though they had a chance to improve the productive techniques of arms and warship from Europe, they invasived Korea which was a country to give them culture and civilization from ancient era, and they plundered the most of treasures of culure for about 36 years. As readers find in Cheonboogyung, Korean have had special moral and philosophical idea in which all the creatures are important to be revered and to make orthers benefit, so we Korean have lived with the idea to serve for all human beings of this world so far. In this point of view we can understand that the reason why the great structure made of big stones as the old fortress can not be seen in Korean peninsula and old Manchuria.

天符經	Cheonbugyung, translated directly
一始無始一	1 begin not begin 1
析三極無盡本	bend 3 pole not away origin
天一一地一一 人一一	heaven 1 1 earth 1 1 human 1 1
一積十鉅無匱化三	1 amass 10 big not(no) out change 3
天二三地二三人二三	heaven 2 3 earth 2 3 human 2 3
人三合六生七八九	big 3 plus 6 bear 7 8

| 運三四成環五七 | move 3 4 become circle 5 7 |

一妙衍萬往萬來用變不動本	1 unbelievably change to all, all became to be used to change without changing origin
本心本太陽昻明人中天地一	origin mind origin big light to be bright human, cosmos and earth become 1
一終無終一	1 end not end 1

For readers, I will introduce some interpretations with modern meaning, but many scholars in Korea do not show the unified opinion to exlain the numbers written above, because as you see, numbers have special metaphysical meanings. Only that I can show you is general opinion which most scholars have had, as the idea of Korean's Cosmology and Ontology coming down from ancient era.

a) Key numbers[56]

1. has the image of the heaven [ultimate being, energy, spirit, cosmos: God],
2. has the image of the two factors of alternation [**Taegeug, yin and yang**: the second one which is followed to 1: earth]
3. has the image of something produced by 2. [materials, some results from alternation, some body born from parents]

1 1. [double 1] has the image of the relation of itself [the state and identity of subject with object, simultaneity and androgyny.]

2 3. has the image of the alternation itself and result of alternation [yin and-yang and result of alternation, next generation]

big 3. has the image of heaven, earth and human.

4.5.6.7.8.9. has the image of functions of alternations followed by big3's alternation.

---

56   Choi, MinJa Ph.D, Cheonboogyung, mosineun saramdeul, 2006, some part of the crux of "Cheonboogyung" translated by Choe, Sukoun,/ writer

b) To transfer to modern image[57]

1 is the origin of this world, but beginning 1 is not absent.
If divided to 3, origin never being fade out.
Heaven, earth and human all have yin and yang.
1 become all, without disappearance of 3.
Heaven, earth and human alternate each other
Big 3 above, alternate together, and become world and universe
Move 3 4, become circulation with 5 7.
1 unbelievably become all, and come and go,
Be useful change but no origin alternated.
Original mind be origin of utmost bright,
With cosmos and earth, human become 1,
With reverence to be brightness.
1 will be finished, but never ending 1.

c) Interpretation in brief

I dare think that this Cheonboogyung might be a stem scripture of all scriptures in this world, to be main stream of ideas in our human history, which make the Way[Dao, truth] brighten, that three essences of universe Cheon, Ji, and In [Heaven, Earth, Human] become one. [This might be similar idea of 'three hypostasis in one ousia' in Greek, which became the basic idea of the trinity theology of the Catholicism.] Here, one means the ultimate power of energy, the reality of God from which heaven, earth(the other beings but human) and human is derived, and three essence of Cheon, Ji, and In are not just mean the reality but mean some alternation or function to harmonize with the others, so we can said that the idea of three-one Ghost, which is the idea coming down from era of 6-7000 years ago to Korean.

The principle of Cheonboogyung, deriving three from one and becoming three to one, is based on the idea that all lives came from one root, and that they must go to one root. As this root is the origin of all in the universe, and the only diety with monotheism idea but which is scattered to all beings, that

---

[57]   Choi, MinJa Ph.D, Cheonboogyung, mosineun saramdeul, 2006, some part of the crux of "Cheonboogyung" translated by Choe, Sukoun,/ writer

is truly only God not for extra religion but for all the beings. Thus the specifity of diety called spirit and Hanullim[God] that exists in and out the small beings and in the universe in common, which we can understand with the number of 1 as written in Cheonboogyung, because 1 never have any branches of personality, but have only common image of trunk of beginner and creator. So I dare insist that this idea of Cheonboogyung can be great answer to the questions to the problems which adressed in front of human beings.

From these idea, another main doctrine of 'make others benefit' have been coming down from ancient era to Korean people. In fact, in our history, though we had had been strong, we did never invade other countries, but only handed over civilization and culture to neighbor countries. For example, our ancestor had taught the way how to agriculture grains to the old Chinese, and the literary and the way how to make ceramics to the Japanese. That have been the mental root of Korean from ancient era.

10

New morality for new era

Morality is the practical characteristics of truth, if the morality were distorted, the truth ought to be distorted in that society. Truth ought to have beautiful complete orderly system, this system is not order made by human, but hamornization formed with all beings in nature. Though this order might be seen some times as chaos partially, but it make beautiful harmony in the higher world of orderly system, which have the character of forward-life-preservation and forward-life-creation, it is just the morality of the active idea and assertive action for accomplishing this beautiful orderly world. Accordingly the identity of morality is not selfish but mutual helpful complimentary value and sometimes altruistic, self-abnegating, selfless value. To tell the truth, this value is seen not only human society to be educated, but all the natures which is created of mam-factors, God's factors in physical world.

We have met many leaders of religions in the world, who have had said that it is righteous that the action to deny other religion might get some moral value and reality of truth in order to keep and to spread their religion, but such a idea is dangerous to lead partial orderly system of the unhappy, anti-life, unnatural world of inharmonious dogma for group selfish, in this cosmos. We human live with the moral identity of good and bad, and we want our children to know good from bad, and right from wrong, but what the standard to differentiate good and bad is. Now our world need some moral standard about this for the hopeful new era. If we identify the good to be forward-life-preservative virtue, bad must be a opposite idea. If we choice selfish value first of all, we will drop down to the evil, but if we make harmonization with others first value, that must be a good according to the law of natural, God's will. The image of good and bad is the idea to belonging to the result of action, not purpose, so there is no the idea of good and evil without any action logically. We occasionally find that the result is not good though somebody act with the good purpose, but it can never be good that some action have done with bad purpose. In this world there is only the bad due to the necessary bad to live of oneself, but human is the only being to act with the bad purpose for greed. This greed become a bigger one in group gathering with same greedy people. This is the original reason of destruction of nature order of truth and of beautiful harmony of Hanullim, God. Ultimately to rescue this world, we have to press one's over greed, and it will be accomplished when the idea get to spread over the world. Through this idea, we can understand Jesus' speach that "I will build church on you Peter." in Bible. If you were God, what do you think thus greed human's action to have had been distorted for long times over about 2,000 years after Jesus' death. Here, let's remember the sentence, "I have had tried but nothing accomplished." which was written by Suwoon with a massage from God. But in Bible, we can see the words of Jesus "I accomplished all." before his death, but after that accident, the history of human beings have had flown to the opposite direction to the way which he have had wanted. About this problem of morality, God [Spirit, Haullim] give us honourable answer via Suwoon again, that miserable method of pray with the sentence of 21 letters. He said that if you pray with reciting this letters loudly or silently with the heart of sincere, reverence and faith, your mind shall be a state of pure spiritual heart, and you shall have moral standard of God [great spirit of cosmos, nature, Haullim] naturally. And at last you shall become honorable saint man and you shall live long. This is the utmost bright standard of morality which shall be given to you. In nature, one can not find any borderline between things and things, but only harmoniztion, just like a short story written below.

There are three drops of water in mediterranean sea, one drop said to another you are not water because you came from Israel, and another drop said that you are not water as well, because you came from Palestine, the other drop of water listening their argument question to them, "What about you all in the sky before becoming rain drop?"

Yes we are all clear blue water drops to flow down to the ocean of truth, if we can discard our greeds, we must be more happy, more comfortable, and more peaceful, and we humankind must recognize that the responsibility to make this earth and cosmos the most comfortable star to live with the neighbours as a excellent being who have the highest spirit given by God.

11

Where we shall go to

Many a teacher of mankind have had told us that we have to get rid of 3 kind of greed for money, fame and power. We can identify greed to be over degree than proper amount needed to live with honesty which God allowed. But due to the base of those mind, our heart becomes greedy and change to the extreme egoism. We human kind know that the origin of murder, terrorism and war is belonging to the egoistic mind. Mind is different from heart, and heart is spirit of us given from God's spirit. We simply live without thinking that if one have spirit, the opposite have it, as well. If some body killed others, it must be the same as killing his own spirit, and his heart became change to the heart of material because all the life has same spirituality just as the identity of God. But, in fact, many men want to rescue of himself after killing God, and to be rich after making God poor, how foolish they are! After such a foolish act, we human hope to go somewhere after death, where might be comfortable and happy more than this life, but we can't sure, so we have to get some religion he propose our hopeful future with reasonableness, not with imagination and group's egoism. But this human's unreasonable expectation had made unreasonable history of human kind, so from this era we have to think more reasonably, more scientifically and more logically according to the development of modern civilization. I dare think that the way of our thought might be righteous to God's will, the truth of the alternation of cosmos, and the truth of nothing of no return. I wrote that the space is the amount of increasing mam-factor and the time is the numbers of increasing mam-factor, so in cosmos, it might be impossible to go back in time and to shrink in space except near inlet space of whirling area of cosmic electro-magnetic stream, if we guess this whirling area it might be getting back in time and in space. But we and other lives, and materials are belong to alternation on the earth, which is simple stage of II dimension of time/space graph figured below, in which all they are positive alternation period as the diagram showed.(ref: time/space graph) Only as a small part of these cosmos, like a dot or light of spark, we come and live on the earth, one of planet revolving round the sun, in our milky way galaxy, during our health going on.

If we could draw such relationship between body and spirit in II dimension graph with mam factor's hypothesis, it may be showed as below.

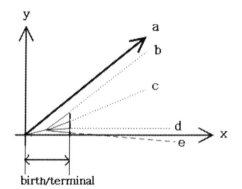

y : space (increasing total volume of mam-factor)

x : time (increasing count of mam-factor)

patterns of future after death

Graph: According to the patterns how to live, one's future shall be determined.

a: increasing amount and count of mam-factors (time+space)
b: absolute pure heart of Jesus and Suwoon (same spirituality with God, eternal life of spirit, parallel to a.)
c: individual pattern of moderate virtual man (moderate spirituality)
d: individual pattern of egoistic man (low spirituality, no helping others)
e: individual pattern of moral hazard man (ghost state)

According to the patterns how to live, one's future shall be determined, just as Newton's physical theory of movement should be adopted, in nature, there may be no other truth which influence to our next world.

We can choice only one curve of upper graph according to our spiritual act during our life, and the result after death only shall be followed as we had done in our life. In fact, we have had lived in the space of three dimensional world, but with thought of time which human can never recognize with limited capability of knowledge, it would be think that we live in the four dimensional world. Time is special concept to be understood by the man who recognize the trace of natural alternation, for example, getting old, growing, changing season etc. If we have another concept that the origin of those alternation, which is invisible extreme fine factor, and if the factor have monopolic life character, electromagnetic specificity with the movement of fluid dynamics, and if they are full in the substance and universe, we can commune with all the lives, materials in the universe through this beings. If we call them spiritual mam-factor as fifth dimensional world, we can said that we live in the five dimensional world. And all the change of universe containing many a galaxies, black hole, big bang and creation of universe is a result of alternation of the greatest amount of this spritual mam-factor ultimately. At last, as well we human being came from ultimate energy of mam-factors of cosmos as the first bit of our heart in our fetus period of our body which was given by our parents and ancestors, as we shall go to the invisible worlds of fifth dimensional, spiritual, ultimate energetic world of mam-factors, proportionally to the result of act which we had done in our life. New philosophical theory, physical hypothesis originated to Donghak theology embracing old theology of all the religions, which was evidenced with the doctrine of Suwoon who learned the truth from God, will become a unification theory of two idea of spiritualism and materialism, and this universe can be understood with the greatest being composed from mam-factor, spiritual components as the first origin of all the materials and universe. And at last, we human beings can commune with all the lives and materials in the world if we want and if we try with the holy God's spirit. Above all, we do never forget the clause showed in lord prayer which was taught by Jesus "...thy kingdom come as it is in heaven...", and another clause was said by Suwoon "...I will make you long live..." These two sentences which showed by God via the Holy two men, might have the greatest image that it is most important to live at peace with neighbors in this world not to go to heaven another world after death. Upper sentence might be understood with my thought that written above, to be born as a man is very hard with the mathematical and biological reliability less than to get spirit which is filled in the universe with my hypothesis, and with Suwoon's doctrine. Now We have to recognize that upper two saint men had emphasized, that not where we shall go to after death, but the way how to live, all the image of heaven and hell might be a metaphor to make man live with honesty and pure mind which state of spirit might be same state of God's spirit. It is truth that our spirit shall go to the proper alternation state in cosmos just to be adapted to our act during our lives as upper graph showed. If somebody had acted virtually during his life, his spirit will return to the way to be parallel with direction of time/space which is cosmic alternation of God's will after losing body, and if anybody had done greedy action during his life, his spirit will go to the way to be down curved to the direction of time/space which is far from God's will, cosmic way of alternation. Now we all can know that our body originate to our parent and ancestor as the vessel in which spirit, mam- factor is put, and so for living it is righteous that all the lives are monolithic existence, and after death they must be thought as if dualistic existence, but at last in the point of mam factor's hypothesis, they are all monolithic beings in the world of unified cosmos.

Key words of Donghak scripture

1. Shichunju: This word showed with the first term of main Jumoon written above means all beings have spirituality of God from the time of birth, and one ought to alternate to the direction of preservation one's life around environment. This doctrine of Donghak is the most important idea critically different from Christianism which have taught. With this doctrine, we can understand the word of 'naeyu-shinryung, waeyu-kihwa' which means that all being in nature is having spirit in and having alternation out, and this doctrine of Suwoon must have great significance to understand the reality and the identity of God with not only theologically but physically and ecologically. This revolutionary doctrine in ontology and in epistemology which was taught by God, will give us new horizon of true value different from old value of past era, and new virtue to be harmonized with others and with natural beings will make our future peaceful and bright. Ultimately it will become beautiful world to live, and we can feel the kingdom of God on the earth as Lord prayer that Jesus said.

2. Honwon-ilki: means the greatest one power of energy which is filled in whole universe. This utmost energy being origin of creation and alternation become one with spirit and truth, which is taught to Suwoon by God, Suwoon said.

3. hurryung-changchang: means the state of universe to be filled with non-seen spirit. Usually hur means the state of empty, but sometimes it means 'invisible state' for example 'hutgeot' means invisible something like ghost in Korean, and **ryung** means spirit, so hurryung is 'invisible spirit'. and changchang means the state of to be full in the space. If we think with insight of this doctrine, we can estimate 'spirit' is not abstractive one but

some being having substancial specificity. All that above written, my hypothesis, could be explored on the basic concrete of this doctrine.

4. Dongkwee-ilchae: means the truth that all beings have to return to one body together. Suwoon used this term at the poem for women, so it might be thought that he might hope to explain the truth of 'nothing of no return' easier for women, or all beings in this world shall return to the origin of creation, God.

5. Muwee-ihwa: means alternation of one's environment to accomplish one's needs or goal naturally without action of selfish. To reach this state, one must have pure mind without any greed through continuous controlling mind, until becoming baby's heart and to be natural state of heart. Similar meaning sentence that we can see in bible, is "See that birds on the sky, they can live with the carefreeness!"

6. Myungdeok-myungdo: This sentence being one clause of Suwoon's 8 poems, means "The bright virtue command you to do the right way." This clause have great significance of Suwoon's doctrine, because the term of **myungdeok** meaning 'bright virtue' is a metaphor of God's will of benevolence and charitableness to all beings, and **myungdo** means that God command us to do the virtue as God do to all beings like a relation of sun to all. Here, we can find the same 'moral command' to 'the categorical imperative' of Kant. About this I had written in the chapter of 'Philosophical approach' above. I think that the image of virtue could be derived from the logical specificity of relationship between creator and creatures, in this relationship. We can never find any differentiations according to the creatures, that image the virtual equality meaning myungdeok having same image of 'categorical' term of Kant. In fact, we can know that I. Kant was a theist having the idea of anti-christianism of his era. But if we think insight with Bible it can be understood that the true image of virtue of God can be found from the relationship between creator to creatures, and creatures to creatures. For example, we can see the sentence of th below in bible, "I tell you that if two of you on earth agree about anything you ask for, it will be done for you by my father in heaven. For where two or three come together in my name, there am I with them. [Mathew 18:19-20]" We can understand from this word of the Bible and from Suwoon's scripture, the true virtue is among the relations between existences. And we have to agree that Jesus, Kant and Suwoon, three

greatest men in our history, all they said only this act will be virtuous, and it is commanded by God, a imperative by pure reason and a fatal identity of consciousness of our heart, Hanullim.

7. Sunggyung-woesim: means basic state of our mind which we have to get our mind to reach the ideal pure heart enough to act with upper virtuous state of Myungdo[the way of heaven]. Sung means the state of mind of utmost sincerity, gyung means the state of mind of utmost reverence, and woe means the mind state of some fearful emotion to the greatest energy of universal power of truth. sim means our mind which we live with. Accordingly this clause of Sunggyung-woesim will become the standard heart of which state we have to try to reach, and so we can understand Suwoon's doctrine of 'training mind to become baby's heart' [ref: susim-junggi] under the theory of shicheonju[ref: **Nonhakmoon**; living state of 'spirit-in, energy alternation-out' of all lives].

Truly it could be said that we can live at peace only with the thought that what we can do for our neighbors, and numerous spiritual animals and plants which have had given their lives for our living. And truly we can make our selves glad when we make others glad. Such a world to be formed with and by those people, can be called 'thy kingdom on earth.'

Only we can expect this world can be accomplished by the acknowledgments of truth that all the lives have same spirit as God, Hanullim with which we can commune with. Please You bless yourself, neighbours and all natural beings with sincerity, reverence and faith!

I give great thanks to readers who read this book to the end page, and to my father, Yeonsoo Choe who showed me the Donghak doctrine through Jumoon and good manner in my boyhood, and give thanks to my wife Choe, Hyosun, who have believed and followed me in spite of many difficulties to live on. Lastly I give thanks to Miss Jaymee Cruz and other staffs in Partridge publishing company who have helped me to make this book.

Printed in the United States
By Bookmasters